SACRED NUMBER
AND THE
ORIGINS OF CIVILIZATION

"Books such as this must be read if we are to hold back the New Dark Ages. Heath's book is profound and the product of years of study and thought. These things have been kept from us by institutional forces and preserved in secret. Only an understanding of these principles can save us."

ROBERT TEMPLE, AUTHOR OF
ORACLES OF THE DEAD AND
THE SIRIUS MYSTERY

SACRED NUMBER
AND THE ORIGINS OF CIVILIZATION

The Unfolding of History
through the Mystery of Number

RICHARD HEATH

Inner Traditions
Rochester, Vermont

Inner Traditions
One Park Street
Rochester, Vermont 05767
www.InnerTraditions.com

Library of Congress Cataloging-in-Publication Data
Heath, Richard.
  Sacred number and the origins of civilization : the unfolding of history through the mystery of number / Richard Heath.
     p. cm.
  Includes bibliographical references and index.
  ISBN-13: 978-1-59477-131-6 (pbk.)
  ISBN-10: 1-59477-131-6 (pbk.)
  1. Numeration—History 2. Number theory—History. 3. Civilization, Ancient. I. Title.
  QA141.2.H43 2007
  513.509—dc22

                                                          2006030011

Printed and bound in the United States by Lake Book Manufacturing

10 9 8 7 6 5 4 3 2

Text layout by Jonathan Desautels
This book was typeset in Sabon with Felix used as a display typeface

The following figures were created by the author using Google Earth maps as their base: 4.18, 4.19, 5.4, 5.5, 5.6, 5.8, 5.9, 5.10, 6.1, 6.8, 6.10, 7.3, 10.1, 10.2, 10.3, 10.4, 10.5, 10.6, 10.7, 10.10, 10.11, 10.12, 10.14, 10.15, and 10.16.

Figures 8.1 and 8.2 are courtesy of Wikimedia Commons, GNU Free Document License. For a copy of the GNUFDL license go to http://en.wikipedia.org/wiki/GNU_Free_Documentation_license

To send correspondence to the author of this book, mail a first-class letter to the author c/o Inner Traditions • Bear & Company, One Park Street, Rochester, VT 05767, and we will forward the communication.

CONTENTS

ACKNOWLEDGMENTS

This book is the product of a wide range of ideas, and a sequence of very productive coincidences. Many of the ideas utilized to build the bigger picture are the result of John Michell's investigations into subjects such as the ancient science of numbers or metrology, centrism, twelve-tribe nations, Jerusalem, and the Michael Lines. John Neal has provided a complete systematic approach to the metrology that has been crucial in the identification of monumental designs such as Carnac and Washington, D.C. Robin Heath's re-discovery of Britain's large landscape triangles and megalithic techniques and units of measure has enhanced and enabled my approach. Howard Crowhurst provided AAK *(Association Archeologique Kergal)* data on Carnac and hosted a guided tour in kilometers. Paul Broadhurst's books confirmed the significance of the Michael Lines, which formed a major thread of historical investigation. Tom Graham's grid for Bornholm gave me a vital clue to the metrology there. Rick Campbell's website on Washington, D.C. identified the basic pattern. Robert K. Temple's persistence in studying oracles and hexagonal geometries helped focus on root three as a unifying phenomenon.

My step daughters, Jessica and Joanna, helped by living in places that led to valuable results in Crete and Cathar country. The DuVersity enabled me to connect to Chartres and Carnac through leading the

"Enchanted Albion" tour with Anthony Blake. A brief stint doing tours at Rosslyn Chapel and other Celtic Trails brought me into the crazy world of Templar-related mysteries such as the Rose Line meridian.

Wikipedia has to be praised for making so much more possible for research and the efficient checking of facts. Google Earth might have been invented specially for this book, for the provision of effective visualizations of landscape geometries and also for providing land measurements that would otherwise require specialist maps and much more labor. Thanks to Anthony Blake for intelligent readings and dialogue throughout.

Thanks also to Robin Heath for copyediting his review manuscript and to Inner Traditions for publishing this work. Finally my wife, Jane, has to be commended for supporting an interminable process of research that appears only now to have been conclusive.

INTRODUCTION
NUMBER AND CREATION

A corpus of ancient knowledge lies behind many of the world's historical cultures—and, in fact, provides a foundation for our modern culture—even though we no longer share the worldview that produced it. In this prehistoric culture the world was seen as a *manifestation of numerical powers*. The ancients worked out a system that described the whole world and cosmos numerically and deduced that it had been created by a recognizable intelligence; this assumption gave birth to religious speculations that literally sought to reconnect to the source of it all. This book will explore the protoculture for which this was the organizing idea, which has become popularly known as "Atlantis."

Two things that are expected when Atlantis is mentioned will, however, not be found here. There is almost no discussion of where Atlantis may have existed and there is also scant mention of the catastrophes that were said to have destroyed it. While there are numerous books with many versions of where Atlantis was and how it was destroyed, this work emerged instead from the identification of specialized cultural material that can only have come from a source such as Atlantis. This cultural material is numerically based.

Numerical knowledge does not rely on the noisy channels of history, archaeology, ancient languages, artifacts, myths, scripture, and so on.

Like the phoenix, it is perfectly reconstructible because number itself is a set of eternal archetypes. Indeed, if the ancients had a numerical science, then numbers are its operators and these have essentially not been damaged by the passage of time. Provided as we are with sufficient clues surviving from the past, then the ancient science is to a great extent a self-reconstituting whole once the area that it dealt with has been exposed.

This book is an overview based upon the ongoing work of just a few people engaged in different aspects of this reconstruction, in order to see what the ancient science might have looked like and how it was then transformed during the historical period. I introduce the subject matter with this theme in mind, and more detailed sources provide a necessary further resource on each of the subjects covered, as mentioned in the footnotes.

This reconstruction can itself be seen as an emerging science, or *proto-science,* which, like all such, is well expressed as being "an elephant in the dark." Different people form different views based upon their perspective, methodology, and so on, some touching the tail, others sensing the breath, and others studying the sound. Thus the work being done to recover the original and objective system of prehistoric thought includes parts of religion, science, art, traditional stories, calendric practices, sacred geography, ideas held by fringe groups, oracular techniques, and so on.

This side of human nature, that can work with higher energies of consciousness and creativity, is perpetually in the dark, a "cloud of unknowing" and a "dark night of the soul." Those that ridicule it are evidently just not drawn to it. The secret is to be able to see in the dark, where no one wants to look. Cultures define themselves by what is illuminated and what is in darkness. One cannot deny therefore the simple equation that new knowledge—which in this case happens to be old knowledge—will not initially seem attractive. Between religious belief and scientific certainty lies a region in which *new* beliefs and great *uncertainties* exist. This is uniquely an area of *human* work in that something new can arise, something latent that connects with the cosmic principle of creation and creativity.

The advantage of focusing on the *numerical cultural traditions* of prehistory is that, within the world of number, there are factual manifestations such as musical harmony, aesthetic proportions, astronomical periodicities, known ancient measures and monuments built with them, and geometrical archetypes.

In the dark ages that followed the destruction of Atlantis, however, the numerical powers that the ancient culture understood as giving rise to all creation became symbolized as gods. The early historical period became filled with symbols, iconographies, and myths that were *degenerate components of the numerical worldview*. Numerical realities were characterized by association to corresponding objects and human characteristics. Scholars have identified storm gods, fertility gods, trickster gods, and so on, but not the system that lay behind them. This has been extraordinarily confusing, for it has meant that scholars could get lost within a system of signs and symbols that often led them to the conclusion that the ancients engaged in a massive pathetic fallacy, that is, that they were "superstitious savages."

On the other hand, out of prehistory we see some of the grandest physical systems, in the form of pyramids and circles made of large (mega) stones (liths), which display an exactness in form and number that does not fit with highly superstitious tribal behavior or within a simplistic pathetic fallacy. A more plausible explanation of megalithic constructional achievement is to suggest that an elite *cadre* of special priests or druids built the monuments, employing a complex tradition of which the ordinary folk only saw a special version. However, this explanation still begs the question of what these builders' traditions were and what part they played in the life of their culture.

The numerate elites of prehistory have become falsely associated with a superstitious general populace more appropriate to a dark age. The fact is, we have very little evidence of the ritual life of prehistory, but a great deal of evidence regarding their numerate skills in the building of monuments. To suggest that a monument is a ritual complex, *without any evidence,* is not scientific. Science has often ignored if not obscured the actual evidence of the monuments having a numerical, metrological, and astronomical basis.

This problem is deepened by the fact that those studying ancient monuments on behalf of official science are rarely trained in the numerate skills that will be shown later to be parts of the Atlantean corpus. This must include archaeologists who until recently resisted the astronomical interpretation of sites and still resist all but the simplest metrological measurements and design hypotheses within the built heritage of megalithic monuments.

In any case, to judge a *high civilization* primarily by its weakest members or most basic activities makes no sense whatsoever. The presentation of savages alongside Stonehenge—such as in the video, *Stonehenge, A Journey Back in Time*—is really unscientific propaganda aimed at marginalizing the numerical culture of a profound prehistoric past.[1]

Why is the numerical culture of the past an anathema to science? This denial of Atlantis has good reason, for the fall of Atlantis *represents closure on an important period of human evolution* that went from a *Stone Age culture* in which humans learned to count, often using marks on bones to track Moon time, to an *Advanced Neolithic culture* that was megalithic, in which the view that the world was a numerical creation led to a culture that measured the world and was capable of building according to the same principles.

The suppression of Atlantis by modern science comes from the instinctive recognition that the modus operandi are fundamentally different now. Science can't imagine an alternative to itself and yet, at root, any science is just a discipline that is applied to a certain kind of problem. Modern science came about when it became possible to properly study physical causation. Eventually these studies eliminated complex dogmas that spirits and invisible forces made things happen. Physical laws were articulated to explain phenomena that had just been curiosities before an organizing principle was identified.

However, I would suggest that the numeracy that modern science employs so well is a direct legacy of an earlier numerical culture. Numerical phenomena drove the development of the older, Atlantean, science. Almost certainly, it was the astronomical time periods and counting that created in ancient people an awareness of number as an organizing principle. This became the earliest form of abstract knowledge.

Structures like Stonehenge and the Great Pyramid can be compared to "big science" particle accelerators or large array radio telescopes, since in all of these, *form* is seen to follow *function,* and these structures are recognizable as uniquely suited to some purpose. But this insight has remained undeveloped in the case of megalithic structures because the worldview behind them is alien to modern culture. The only language that can reveal the form and function of megalithic structures is that of number, the science of metrology (measurements based on the size and shape of Earth), and alignment.

A more subtle point is that if Atlantis was a necessary stepping stone in human cultural evolution then its destruction appears to have included a *loss of interest* in the use of numbers to define the cosmos.

In the medieval period, prehistoric and non-Christian cultures and beliefs were called "country" or "pagan," just as in the days of the Romans other cultures were called "barbarian," despite the proclivities of the Romans themselves. It is really a natural form of cultural chauvinism that makes it hard to accept the greatness yet difference of the ancients.

In addition to the human suppression of the ancient knowledge referred to as "Atlantean," a physical disappearance of the place itself also occurred. The disappearance of Atlantis belongs alongside many other "falls" related in the myths of humanity:

- the Expulsion of Adam and Eve from Eden
- the Confounding of the Tower of Babel
- the Falling of the World Tree (or a Mill)
- the Fall of Atlantis

These stories contain lost information as alternative versions and related messages. While today "myth" can mean an untruth, there is no doubt that in ancient cultures storytelling was a grand discipline, having exact rules for the preservation of information and language in the ages when written records were not commonly available and hence before "history" became literature.

"The Expulsion of Adam and Eve from Eden" (Genesis 2:3) is a story about a type of knowledge, a "tree of knowledge of good and evil . . . in the midst . . . of the Garden," which means the cosmic knowledge of Earth's axis and the gods. A serpent, traditionally a symbol of a planetary being (probably Mercury), was entwined about that tree and suggested eating the fruit that hung upon its branches.

The fruit that hangs on this tree is knowledge of the numerical relationships between planets that both initiates an understanding of number and reveals that the creation is indeed structured in a numerical way. The numerical culture would eventually measure the size of Earth itself and "become as one of us [the gods], to know good and evil." But when humans become knowledgeable of the cosmic, it angers a God that would keep them within a created paradise or, alternatively, forces a newly self-conscious couple to leave the garden paradise and make their own way in the world.

"Confounding the Tower of Babel" (Genesis 11:4–5) is a remarkably similar story. Here, human beings who speak one language say "let us build us a city and a tower, whose top may reach unto heaven" and "let us make us a name [or culture], lest we be scattered abroad upon the face of the whole earth." This also annoyed the Lord and his solution in this case was to "confound their language" so that they "may not understand one another's speech."

The Tower of Babel was probably a seven-tiered "model of heaven" built according to definite measurements; it represents a megalithic type of structure, even though built of brick as was the practice in Mesopotamia. It appears this city-building civilization was confounded by a change in the way people thought and communicated; it was this that caused misunderstandings and differences to arise. These people seem strangely prescient in predicting their own scattering, *as if it came with the territory*.

"The Falling of the World Tree (or a Mill)"[2] is based upon the conception of Earth's polar axis as a tree trunk and the sky its branches, leaves, and fruit, as in the Eden story, or of the sky's rotation as a Mill, with the planets off-center and Earth's axis as its axle, extensively described in Shakespeare's play *Hamlet*.

This is a mythic frame in which the procession of the equinoxes and major conjunctions of planets were thought to generate what we would call world history, formed of great ages lasting thousands of years, each with their own astrological flavor associated with specific equinoctal and polar stars. This was a ubiquitous prehistoric tradition, preserved in worldwide myth and legend.

"The Fall of Atlantis" (see Plato's *Timaeus* and *Critias*) is of an explicit super-culture destroyed by catastrophe, a story transmitted via Egypt to classical Greeks by Solon, the founder of democratic Athens. This story has a semi-historical character: Unlike the others it speaks directly and offers specific clues as to where and how the previous numerical civilization was brought down by natural forces.

These myths have a uniqueness that ensures their independence from any others—they cannot be amalgamated. They give a set of different perspectives on what could be a single phenomenon: the destruction of a large and well developed culture, which left few traces of its former center. All these myths describe the fall of a culture that *developed a kind of knowledge,* but that was dispersed by a mixture of events—geological, meteorological, political, or psychological.

The knowledge that was developed represented a shift in power within human consciousness regarding innovation. Innovation requires imagination and imagination is of things not present. This *sixth sense* is a dangerous faculty since it can be for good or evil: it can make humans like gods and it can also delude and manipulate.

The problems *caused by imagination* are evolutionary for humanity. They change the role of the human: As an outwardly creative force, the human presence impacts the world. Creatures that effectively can act "as angels" are *in potentio* replacements for the archaic form of creativity built into creation which in Greek is called the *demiurge* or craftsman god (Deus Faber). Indeed this faculty appeared with the smiths and craftsmen of the Bronze Age.

The confounding of language, the catastrophic termination of Atlantis, the expulsion of Adam and Eve from Eden, and the falling of the Sky Mill of world history are thus archaic perspectives on *human changes* that made human beings more active in shaping their environment.

This stage could not have been reached without the precursor that evolved numeracy in a distinctly profound form and discovered that the world was created according to a numerical pattern. But this worldview is essentially static once reached and nothing really different can be created once complete rapport with creation is reached.

These catastrophes need to be understood within a framework in which, on one level, humanity means nothing to higher powers that are effecting evolution, even though it is the human that is being evolved. This is why civilized values will always remain subjective so long as there is not a cosmic objectivity. The corollary to this is that cosmic objectivity cannot evolve but is, like the angels, doomed to remain beyond the domain within which the transformation must occur.

Thus the angels may be jealous of humans, Jehovah angry at Adam's natural reactions, and scientists angry with non-scientists who claim that Atlantis is alive and kicking, not directly as the numerical model of the world but as its numerical legacy in everything we measure in time or space, or in the symbolic roots of myth inherent in our evolved tales of meaning.

Imagination can also introduce errors or misreadings that reveal new valid readings, by seeing things a different way, just as genetic reproduction generates new genes. This power brings the world into a new existence, injects new levels of order—but from where? It may very well be that humanity is in contact with the cosmic forces through the power of imagination and that this is the very mechanism that made the destruction of Atlantis both necessary and worthwhile.

Even though it was destroyed, the ancient protoculture left behind some *prehistoric* monuments that employ a *historical* system of measures, as well as a global corpus of visual and oral traditions, symbols, and mythology. These elements formed the cultural starting points for all the civilizations that have arisen since. We aim to trace the continuing influence of these cultural elements and their ongoing effect within world history. To understand how this is true, recent rediscoveries of number within geocentric astronomy and monumental metrology have first to be presented, the task of the early chapters. These numerical sciences, a golden thread for this story, throw new light on practices found in the antecedents of "Western" civilization.

ONE

NUMBERS FROM THE SKY

The human body experiences a number of cyclic phenomena, the most important being that due to the rhythm of the heart. Longer term, the cycle of sleep and wakefulness causes a range of periodic hormonal effects that alter the metabolism. As a single cell in the body, could one infer the existence of the human body, a greater and highly organized whole, from these rhythms?

This is like our situation as we observe the sky from our planet, where the heart beat is the cycle of day and night, the basic cycle of experience on Earth caused by the rotation of Earth relative to the Sun. The Sun dominates the day to focus visual attention upon all that its light strikes, including the sky, made blue through scattering of that light by molecular particles, punctuated by the clouds made gray by somewhat larger water droplets. The night can be illumined by the Moon, but moonlight is light reflected from the Sun, and varies according to the Moon's position relative to the Sun. The Moon, truly the Queen of the night in all her phases, travels past a starry backdrop that never varies its pattern, the so-called fixed stars and constellations. These must have been the earliest observations.

THE DAY COUNTS

The variation of the Moon becomes an interesting and important phenomenon to people who live largely outdoors, and certainly was such before doors were invented! The fact that the human female reproductive cycle has a natural synchronization to the Moon's phases simply follows a similar resonance in other populations living on Earth. The Moon has also been referred to as the original street lamp and the way it lights the night sky creates a natural month. This cycle of the Moon is a countable phenomenon, a cycle that presents the possibility of knowing how many days will lapse before the Moon will be full again.

The moon does not take an exact number of days to complete its cycle of phases but does so in just over 29½ days. This means that the time for two cycles can be very accurately counted in days, since a full moon will then occur *at the same time of night,* fifty-nine days later.

Inscribed bones from the later Stone Age have been interpreted by Alexander Marshack as having marks that include this two month cycle of counting days (see figs. 1.1 and 1.2).[1] This should perhaps be expected, since Stone Age people were no less bright than ourselves, with a comparable brain size. The capabilities of prehistoric people have remained unproven only because their thinking process and social mores cannot be deduced from present interpretations of archaeological data. However, they can be inferred from artifacts such as these bones.

The carved patterns on prehistoric bones are precedents for the symbols that came to decorate pots, provide borders and friezes, "key patterns" (ornamental patterns consisting of repeated groups of joined vertical and horizontal lines), and a world of design that graces our museums today. Were these patterns originally generated because they could "hold" numerical information? Also, could these patterns be an early form of notation and hence of language, a language initially of counting and direct symbolism with regard to the sky events?

The quantity of decorated bones, stones, pots, and paintings that have a potentially numerical meaning, and the range of the prehistoric period of their origins, indicates that creating symbols of counting was a primary activity of humankind at this time, at least as significant as cave art and other skills. The markings represent a strong signal emanating from that period; where there is a strong signal it can form the starting

Figure 1.1. One of Marshack's lunar counting bones.

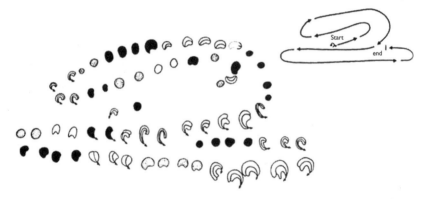

Figure 1.2. Marshack's schematic version of the count.

impulse for a new level of capability, in this case, the ability to work with numbers in the abstract.

What started as a curious counting with impromptu marks may have ended with the idea: "How many Moons are there in a year?" To answer such a question the year has to be observed and its characteristics understood.

A LANDSCAPE OF TIME

Wherever humans have lived for some time at a given location—other than at the equator or in a jungle—the pattern of the year and the impact of its seasons on human life becomes evident in a number of specific ways. Time will then naturally reveal a solar cycle in which the Sun is higher in the sky in summer and lower in the winter.

The effect of the Sun's variation in height manifests as a large and therefore measurable movement of its setting and rising position at the horizon (fig. 1.3). These points of rising and setting, seen from a single vantage point, form the equivalent of notches cut on a bone. The landmarks on the horizon become memorable symbols of, say, the midsummer sunrise point or that of midwinter sunset. Other intermediate points stretch between these midsummer and midwinter alignments to form a natural calendar, symmetrical about east (for sunrises) and west (for sunsets).

The Stone Age, when bone counts were carved, culminated in the megalithic period, during which large stones were used for monumental purposes. It is now commonly accepted that one of the primary languages articulated by these monuments was the notation of the solar alignments at a place in order to define a calendar (fig. 1.4). Monuments found in

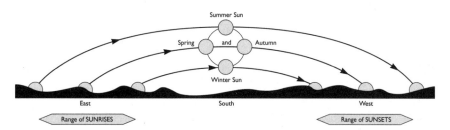

Figure 1.3. The natural calendar of local space formed by the horizon, sunrise, and sunsets during a year.

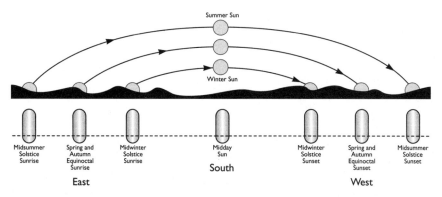

Figure 1.4. The use of stones in circles to mark the natural calendar on the horizon.

Britain and northwest Europe can be anything from a single standing stone to complex stone rings.

The creation of a solar calendar requires a center, formed either by a solitary standing stone or by surrounding a central stone with a circle of stones. The center can then be aligned with one of the surrounding stones or a standing stone in the middle distance or even a feature on the horizon such as a rocky crag. The longer the sightline the more accurate the alignment; the nearer the stone, the more symbolic of that alignment or date it becomes. A symbolic stone forms an *aide memoire,* near at hand, of the cosmic phenomenon.

While the culture of the megalithic is long gone, the monuments and their alignments remain. Though still enigmatic to science, the alignments demonstrate knowledge of the sky and a high degree of competence in the measurement of angles both in the sky and on the land. This means that the observation of the sky had intensified the skill of counting, through marks, into a capacity to measure angles.

If the Moon cycles in a year are counted, it soon becomes clear that there are over twelve lunations (lunar months) in a year. The "over" equals very nearly one third of a lunation. This means that in three years there are twelve + twelve + twelve + one extra lunations, making thirty-seven in all. This three year period is a strong contender for the origin of the concept of "threeness" associated with the Moon in Celtic times (fig. 1.5).

During a year, however, the Sun has its highest and lowest positions (called solstices) and two middle positions (called equinoxes), during which day "equals" night. Thus, while the Moon manifests "threeness," the Sun manifests "fourness"—numerically, not symbolically—as, respectively, three years or four positions of sunrise and sunset within the year.

We know from the "Traditional Arts" taught in medieval universities —Grammar, Logic, Rhetoric, Arithmetic, Geometry, Musical Harmony, and Astronomy—that the pre-scientific mind was disposed to see number as arising out of the whole, that is, out of "oneness." Oneness was symbolized geometrically by the whole circle, and both are symbolic of the concept of eternity, since cycles tend to repeat without end of time.

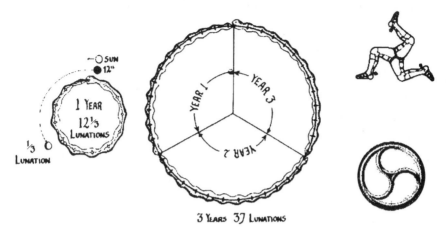

Figure 1.5. The natural three-fold cycle of the Moon and some of the consequential symbolism from the Celtic world.

Nowhere can the prototype of this perception be found as clearly as in the sky and the circuits of the stars, the Sun, Moon, and planets. It is natural therefore to see number as being part of an eternity, as cosmic cycles divide into each other, as with days into a month and months into a year.

Each cosmic time period is a whole, characterized by what other cycles do within it. The circuit of the stars by night and of the Sun by day echo the rotation of Earth, both being caused by that rotation. However, the movement of the Moon, night by night, and of the planets follows a different circuit, that we today call the zodiacal belt or ecliptic. These two circuits—of rotation and planetary orbital motion—are separated from each other because Earth's north–south axis is tilted relative to the Sun and planets. This is a fact of fundamental importance.

THE TOPOGRAPHY OF HEAVEN

In recent times the zodiac has been divided into twelve parts, though in the past twenty-seven or twenty-eight divisions were also used, called in India the *nakshatras* or "lunar mansions." Any division of the zodiac is made possible by the fixed patterns of the stars behind the Moon at night. It is true to say that the celestial topography of distinct star groups or constellations, recognizable in the sky, is comparable to the topography of Earth's horizon.

This element of topography is connected to the practice of giving names to significant places, which has led directly to storytelling as a mechanism for articulating found meaning within phenomena and events. This mythic tradition from the ancient world has survived in spite of the many processes that have destroyed cultures and their other artifacts. In fact there is today a remarkably rich set of myths and place names in many regions, often collected within scholarly compendia. Many such myths relate to the sky, in that the conjunction of gods or heroes and mythic places correspond to celestial events. For example, the book *Hamlet's Mill* implies that:

- planets are referred to in myths as gods,
- stars are referred to in myths as animals (the word zodiac means "dial of animals"),
- topographical descriptions (positions of places in relation to each other) in myths describe the position of the Sun against the fixed sphere of stars.

While these conclusions were derived largely from Old World mythology, the same has been found to also be the key to Andean myth from the New World. William Sullivan applied them to great effect in his research reported in *The Secret of the Incas*. This suggests that a symbolic and linguistic world had already been evolved by megalithic times (4500–1500 B.C.E.), in parallel to the astronomical concerns found in the monuments and their alignment to the sky. This process could have emerged naturally out of the Stone Age period, with its evidence of counting and notation.

Naming is really a superior type of marking, containing levels of meaning not achievable by counting, such as social metaphors that resonate with the human condition and experience, such as male and female planets or gods, stories based upon everyday life, and so on. Just as stories were told beneath cave paintings to animate and enlarge on the storyboards, so sky lore can be told beneath the cave of the sky, as it has been called in more recent but similar cultures.

THE SUN'S COMPANIONS

The most visible planet of all is Venus. Regarded as feminine, she was an ancient goddess and put alongside the Moon and Earth to form a triple goddess. Because they are inner planets, Venus and Mercury are both tied to the Sun and are within Earth's own orbit. Venus has the greater orbit and can easily be seen after the Sun has set. When visible after sunset, she is moving between Earth and the Sun to form the phenomenon called the evening star. After passing by Earth, she can be seen as the morning star before the Sun rises. Most sacred texts including the Bible make much of these phenomena. Along with the crescent moon, waxing by evening or waning by morning, the Venus "star" forms a familiar yet stunning icon used particularly by the Islamic world.

Within our calendar year of 365 whole days, the repetition of the evening star of Venus occurs in an exact numerical relationship of five to eight. That is, dividing 365 by five we obtain a period of seventy-three days that, multiplied by eight, yields the Venus synodic period (time between successive conjunctions of two celestial bodies) of 584 days. In the zodiac, this causes each successive evening star of Venus to appear 2/5 further on in the sky relative to the stars and 3/5 (0.6 of a year) later in the year. When the zodiacal belt is drawn as a circle, the Venus cycle forms a pentagram shape after eight years have elapsed on Earth (fig. 1.6).

Thus the "Venus cycle" is eight years long and involves five complete cycles of Venus phenomena. This is easily deduced just from counting the days, and from knowing the seasons as a calendar naturally created by the Sun on the horizon, never far from an evening or morning star.

This means that fiveness naturally came from the sky to early humans. The pentagram/pentagon evolves another powerful symbol of the ancient world, the Golden Mean, a unique ratio (1:1.618 . . .) whose reciprocal and square all have the same irrational fractional part as the number itself: 0.618 . . . . The Golden Mean is found in Egyptian and Greek temple buildings and is also a template for the proportions of life itself, emerging naturally in the formation of living bodies, including the

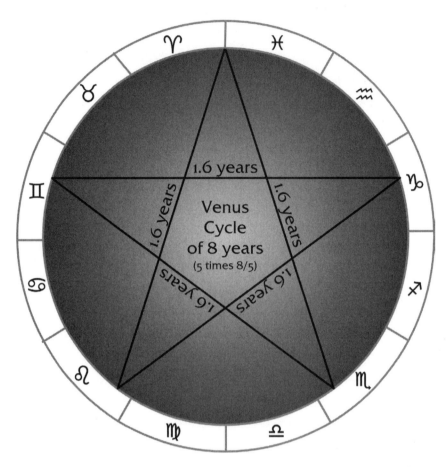

Figure 1.6. The Venus cycle of eight years in which a morning or evening star has five manifestations, dividing the zodiac into a pentagram.

human. The ancient Egyptians left evidence of their canon of proportion within the human body in their meticulous temple drawings, which changed little over thousands of years.

Five is the mathematical root of this Golden Mean ratio, simply demonstrated in that many Golden Mean proportions are to be found within a drawing of pentagram star (fig. 1.7). In this way, five is associated both with living structures and the feminine Venus.

Mercury, the planet closest to the Sun, shares similar evening and morning stardom but it is rarely seen by the uninitiated. Mercury is so close to the Sun that it is often lost in the Sun's light. However, the

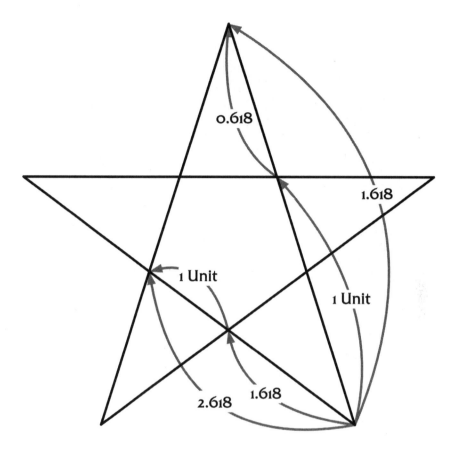

Figure 1.7. A few of the Golden Mean relationships found within the pentagram.

symbolism of Mercury also follows its astronomical behavior. Within a year the synodic period of Mercury, and its repetition of evening and morning stars, generate a Star of David upon the zodiac (fig. 1.8). While not so obvious, sixness does have an association with Mercury, which is confirmed by symbolic developments noted in chapter 7.

Thus the inner planets can be seen to have introduced numerical competence and meaning into the early mind. If one argues the opposite, then the later traditional symbols seem to have come from nothing but arbitrary human imagination. But the global phenomenon of symbolic congruence found within mythical tales requires a general availability of just such number clues, within the general environment of humanity. There is

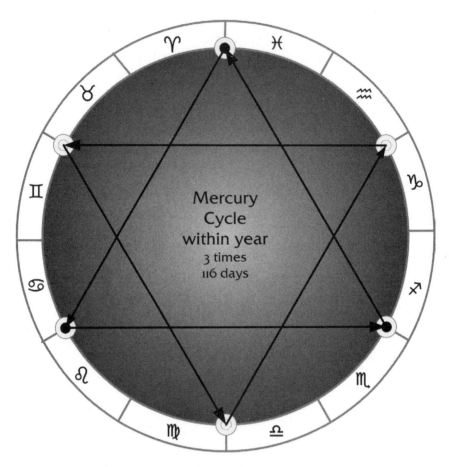

Figure 1.8. The Mercury cycle of inferior and superior conjunctions creates a Star of David figure within one year.

no more available "general environment" than the sky and the behaviors found there.

The meanings of *three, four, five,* and *six* are therefore associated with the Moon, Sun, Venus, and Mercury. The presence of such low numbers within the environment does not end with these bodies; in fact, the whole system of time on Earth is far simpler than one would expect without there being forces at work that prefer smaller numbers. As we will see, resonance is a possible mechanism for this but how the solar system was created may have been irrelevant to early humans. What resonates within the mind are these numbers, because the found time periods "speak" clearly of them.

THE OBSERVING OF CALENDARS

The natural observation of the calendar using horizon alignments leads to the natural tendency for symbols to become independent of what they refer to. A bone with lunar marks can lead to the imagination that in three days the Moon will reemerge from the Sun as an evening crescent. Therefore ancient civilizations are likely to have used various types of calendars based on celestial events.

Calendars are usually lunar or solar. The Muslims and Jews have retained a sacred lunar calendar, which shifts a third of a "month" every year, just as the day of the week shifts a day every year in our solar calendar. Solar calendars can be exact, practical, or conceptual, having 365.25 (almost exact), 365 (practical), or 360 (conceptual) days.

In all calendars, any days or parts of days left over are dealt with by having festival days, weeks, or months that absorb them. However this is done, there is no simple calendar that can simply harmonize the cycles of the Sun and the Moon, almost as if the periods of the two bodies were designed with a high degree of variation, even chaos, in mind.

Most calendars are based on the counting of days, but the lunar month, as we have seen, is not a simple number of days long. Thus weeks do not relate to the months of the Moon, which is why uneven month lengths often creep into a calendar matched to the Sun. In other words, there is great apparent complexity in the calendars familiar to us, whether solar or lunar, in contrast to the phenomena observed to be as simple three, four, five, and six.

The next number, *seven,* provides the key as to why the calendar currently used is so complex. A simpler, original calendar was probably suppressed for religious reasons when the week of seven days observed today was adopted by two well-known cultures. Most famously the Jews start their Pentateuch, or Five Books, with the universe coming into existence in seven stages called days. The Bible, like most sacred literature, contains material from a mixture of cultures in addition to the one that "owns" it. Genesis, for example, includes recognizable elements of Chaldean (that is, Babylonian) stories, such as a version of a world tale, the flood, and the hero who preserves all life in a boat. The Tower of Babel story refers to Babylon. Such transplants could come from periods when the Jews were held in captivity by the Babylonians. Thus, some of their wisdom—and the week—appear to have come from the Magi, the wise men of Babylon.

The classical Greeks also had a week of seven days, which tends to be overlooked because of the influence of Judaism upon Christianity. But in fact the Greeks, especially those from Alexandria, were as influential in the creation of the New Testament scriptures. This can be seen from the influx of numerical mysteries even within the four gospels, written in Greek and employing *gematria,* the ancient science of letter-number symbolism.

The Greek week associated the seven days with the planets, Sun, and Moon, as is shown by our present names for the days such as Saturday (Saturn's day), Sunday (Sun's day), and Monday (Moon's day). The Greek version must either have come south with the Indo-Europeans, or west, probably from the Persian Empire (which Alexander the Great defeated) (fig. 1.9).

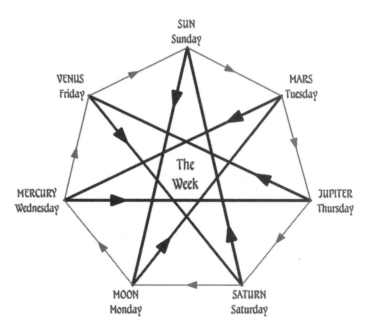

Figure 1.9. The structure of the week where the outer sequence has planets in their order of angular motion, Moon fastest, while the inner lines give the conventional order in the week.

SATURN, GOD OF TIME

Planets are seen from Earth as "wanderers" through the firmament, which is what the word *planet* means. The outer planets are not tied to the Sun like Venus and Mercury are. As Earth passes between an outer planet and the Sun, the planet forms a loop in the night sky, against the stars. Mars, Jupiter, and Saturn all make such loops (fig. 1.10). The period of time between such loops, in which Earth catches up with the given planet's changed position, is what is known as its synodic period.

The loops of Saturn, as they move through the constellations, are separated by about the same angle as the Moon moves in a single day, between nights and against the same constellations. The point here is that the same technology—viewing something against the stars to track its motion—can be applied to these loops, and the counting process of using just the day itself remains identical.

Saturn's synodic period is almost exactly 378 days. This period has the property of being a multiple of seven. Thus, the week of seven days divides perfectly into the 378 days of Saturn to yield fifty-four weeks. Our year is fifty-two weeks long, but not exactly so. It is fifty-two weeks

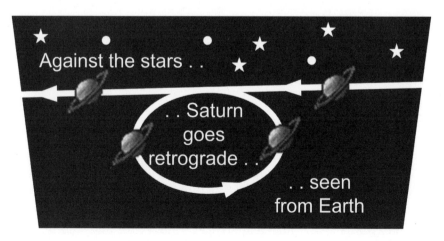

Figure 1.10. As Earth passes between Saturn and the Sun, Saturn appears to go backward (retrograde) and form a loop in the sky. (In practice, the loop is not as open as shown here.)

plus one day long, because 365 days cannot be divided by the seven day week. To compensate, many cultures had a Saturnian year that was "a year and a day" long, that is, 364 days plus one day. These traditions are well documented in cultures that were matrilineal: where the female formed the stable core of the society.[2] In these cultures a titular king reigned for just this year and a day, then was sacrificed to the year, which itself dies only for another to arise.

From the year of 364 days also emanated the number *thirteen*, suppressed as being unlucky, for there are thirteen months of twenty-eight days in 364 days—each month having four weeks of seven days. Such regular months—in contrast with our irregular ones—meant that the calendar was easier to follow without printed versions, or priests to provide reminders.

Another outer planet, Jupiter, has a longer synodic period of 399 days, because it is closer to Earth, moves more quickly, and hence takes longer for the Sun's motion to oppose it. Conveniently, 399 divides by seven also! It seems most unlikely that the only giant planets visible to naked eye observers on Earth should have synodic periods that divide by seven days. This would have seemed a significant fact to ancient peoples. The adoption of a seven day week would naturally be a logical part of any sacred calendar.

Once adopted, the 364/378 day calendar can incorporate Jupiter, whose synod is just twenty-one days or three weeks longer than that of Saturn. Since both synods divide by twenty-one days, this reveals that Saturn is related to Jupiter in the ratio eighteen to nineteen. This is a very simple relationship.

When the lunar year is compared to these two planets, yet more order emerges (fig. 1.11). The lunar year is usually taken to be twelve lunar months, about 354 days. To the Jupiter synod this gives a ratio of 8:9 and to Saturn a ratio of 15:16. Both these two ratios belong to the world of pure musical tone and are called the whole tone and the half tone, respectively. The concept of the "harmony of the spheres" is thus based upon some simple truths. It appears these two outer planets both have a musical relationship to the Moon.

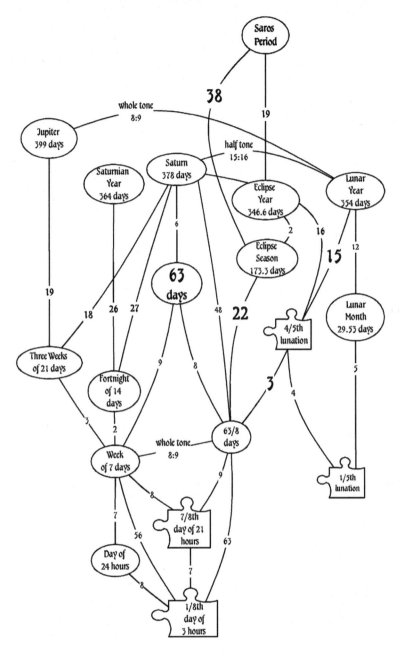

Figure 1.11. Saturnian calendar based on item 2646 from Knossos (a.k.a. "Disk of Chronos"), Heraklion Museum, Crete. The Saturn time periods shown as a chart in which smaller time periods are multiplied to create, exactly, significant longer time periods for the Moon, eclipses, Saturn, Jupiter, and so on. This would have formed a complete calendar, lost today except for the seven day week.

The relationships between the Moon, Saturn, and the eclipses were made clear only by a visit to the Heraklion Museum at Crete and a viewing of an object that the catalog labels "a perforated vessel." I call it the "Disk of Chronos" (fig. 1.12). It consists of a series of holes punched into a clay disk. Its primary motif is a star with seven flames or waves. The outer ring allows the counting of sixty-three days, which period is one sixth of the Saturn synod. The inner ring has fifteen holes, which applies to the 15:16 ratio between the lunar year and Saturn.

This disk leads directly to a very complete, simple yet accurate set of time relations that can track the motion of Saturn, the Moon, and the eclipse seasons as in figure 1.11. A calendar based upon it employs the simplest unit of measure available on Earth, the day. It also employs units based upon the week, because Saturn's period divides perfectly by seven days. Thus, *our present seven day week would be the natural choice for people operating the Saturnian calendar.*

This explains the adoption of the seven day week, both practically, as a calendrical device, and evidentially, as an historical reality predat-

Figure 1.12. The Disk of Chronos. Item 2646 is a "Perforated Utensil" possibly for use with incense. (New Palace Period: Advanced and Final Phase of the Palace of Knossos Gallery V, The Heraklion Museum)

ing classical Greece. This calendar would have been contemporaneous with Egypt and other parts of the Minoan sea-trading network. It may have been the source of the Jewish seven day week: Moses, trained as a priest, and his brother Aaron, might well have heard of this in Egypt, alongside the other knowledge they gleaned, which allowed them to establish the Jewish sacred measures and the metrological language of sacred building (see later chapters).

THE BIRTH OF ZEUS

In the mythology of Zeus, Chronos—Zeus's father, and the god of time—is accused of swallowing his own children. Perhaps we can see in this a reference to a system of time that, if followed, effectively denies (swallows) all the other celestial cycles and planets.* In fact the ancients could have "got hung up" on such a simple system of time. Zeus is saved from such a fate by his mother and is brought up in a Cretan cave, hidden from his father who might hear his cries. This implies that the drama is one being played out in Crete, with Chronos just down the road rather than in some abstract heaven.

Most significantly, Zeus grows up to depose his father and become the god of the classical world from which Western culture has largely evolved. The calendar implicit in the Disk of Chronos evidently fell out of use and was replaced, probably with those for which there are historical records. It therefore seems likely that the overthrow of Chronos by Zeus was related to these calendrical practices and that Chronos was related to some fixed religious regime associated with the older Saturnian calendar. Since the calendar is simpler than it *should be*—that is, because time periods should not match so simply (in days) the periods of Saturn, the Moon, and eclipses—then no further development of time was likely among those living under such a calendar. The god of time would have dominated thought and the religious precincts of the Bronze Age, until deposed and replaced by an Indo-European invasion that

---

*For example, a lunar eclipse is symbolically a "swallowing" of the Moon.

brought its own pantheon of gods, largely preformed, from the Baltic north (see chapter 6).

The clash of the Titans, of the old gods with the new, marked an end to the prehistoric calendar. The stability of prehistory was soon replaced by a Bronze Age dynamism that within centuries would establish the project of written history and scriptures, coinage and money, trade, pillage, and taxation.

Prehistory appears, then, to have been based upon an understanding of number that came quite simply from observing celestial time periods. This naturally equated planets with causative gods. The Greeks and others adopted this symbolism, but it appears that over time this knowledge was lost and the role of the seven day week in Saturn's synodic period was lost with it.

The Saturnian calendar gives us two musical tones that belong to another numerical science, that of harmony. Having understood that numbers were the gods (the planets only being manifestations of number) the ancients might naturally have looked at the nature of the number field and musical harmony, as we shall in the next chapter.

TWO

THE ROOT OF ALL
MEASURES

It is possible that all the complexity in the world has arisen just from the properties of number, despite the apparent nature of numbers as being passive and inactive symbols. Used for recording quantities, numbers have become associated with routine activities such as keeping accounts, or calculating and measuring within the physical and financial worlds.

If numbers are seen as the power of grouping things into different systems or of creating a field of harmony, another side to their nature emerges: numbers then define how things divide into each other, and this inter-division reveals the compatibility of one thing with another. In the previous chapter planetary periods were shown to divide into each other to reveal definite number relationships of this sort.

This ability of one number to divide into another is crucial to an understanding of the individual properties of numbers in the following way: A number that cannot be divided by another number is called a *prime number*. Some early prime numbers are two, three, five, seven, eleven, thirteen, seventeen, and nineteen.

This indivisibility concept is very important and is called *incommensurability,* meaning that one smaller measure *cannot divide* or find its measure within a larger measure a whole number of times. Any fractional part "left over" is today represented as a decimal fraction such as

0.090909, which is far better written as 1/11. In metrology, such fractions are caused purely by the units employed, by what unit is chosen to be divided into another whole. For the number pi, a number that no amount of decimals can fully define, the one or unit is simply the diameter of a circle and pi is then the circle's circumference.

Numbers that are not prime are each divisible by at least two lesser prime numbers. For example, six is divisible by two and by three. This means that in looking at the power of numbers, especially as they were conceived in the ancient world, it is the pattern of the primes and non-primes within the continuum of whole numbers that provides both a master plan and the part in that plan of any individual number.

THE THEORY AND PRACTICE OF NUMBERS

As already shown, numerical relationships probably revealed themselves to the ancient mind through the counting of astronomical periods. In the case of the week and the Saturn calendar, it is obvious that the number seven is highly apparent in the structure of time on Earth. Given what is now known about the science of metrology that then developed in the ancient world, we can confidently say that the missing link between the later metrology and the original counting of number is *the discovery of the field of number itself* and its properties.

This study of number would today be classed as pure mathematics, largely in a field called "number theory," long relegated as a specialized field known only to mathematicians. What is likely to have occurred within the prehistoric setting, though, is the growth of educational institutions that taught and developed the knowledge of astronomy, musical harmony, and Earth measure. In them this core subject of number theory would have been the fundamental language of how numerical structure comes into existence.

Sacred buildings have always been based upon number. However, megalithic structures are today looked upon as ceremonial and little else. Our modern prejudices preclude looking for educational purpose, yet modern researchers, such as those who have studied the metrology of the structures, have themselves *learned* a great deal. This implies, ipso facto, that even without having megalithic instructors available, these structures remain and *have been* educational in recent times.

The subjects taught at a megalithic university must have held a close relationship to the traditional arts that were taught in the medieval universities. The medieval student needed to master seven disciplines to be considered educated (fig. 2.1). The first group of three—

Figure 2.1. Septem Artes Liberals *(the Seven Liberal Arts) from* Hortus deliciarium *of Herrad von Landsberg (circa 1180).*

Grammar, Logic, and Rhetoric—prepared the student for rational thought. They were called the *Trivium* in Latin as they were considered "trivial" compared to the four mathematical arts of Arithmetic (number theory), Geometry, Musical Harmony, and Astronomy. These latter subjects, called the *Quadrivium,* were those required to build the megalithic monuments.

While the counting of astronomical time periods revealed that numbers have properties and developed geometrical competence, the field of number provided the foundation for all these numerical sciences. From this foundation a full numerical worldview would have been possible, one that found its fullest expression within the design, location, and structure of ancient monuments.

Metrology became the medium for applying this number knowledge to Earth itself, its size and shape, and the location and design of the monuments built upon it. Metrology appears to have been the most sophisticated product of the ancient world, a quintessence of the other four mathematical arts, drawing upon them through the alignments, geometry, proportions, and harmony built into ancient monuments.

THE FOUNDATION NUMBERS AND MUSICAL HARMONY

Socrates and Lao Tzu paraphrase each other in saying that the whole of creation is based upon one (the whole), two (the division of it), and three (the interrelation of parts). In some way all else was said to follow from these three. Indeed, the next number that does not divide by two or three is also a prime number (four does not qualify since it is the first square number, two times two).

The field of number starts with the number one. Indeed its *character* is created by the number one, since every integer number like two or three is whole like one yet divisible into a number of ones. Even the idea of one God might have sprung from this property of the number field. Today, the integers are thought to be irrelevant primitives compared to the complex fractions involved in calculations of system dynamics and statistics, but from the ancient perspective this is just the blindness of not having had a proper mathematical foundation.

Musical harmony arises between the most fundamental of numbers: one through six (fig. 2.2). Two is the octave relationship of 1:2 (that is, "doubling") with respect to one, and three forms the perfect fifth of 2:3 (that is, "two to three") with two. Four then becomes another octave relationship to two, which is the same as 1:2 because 2:4 can be divided by a common factor, two. This is an important principle, that *musical ratios are the irreducible elements* with any common factors taken out. Four also ushers in the prototype of the perfect fourth, 3:4, the next most harmonious musical proportion. Combined with the fifth (2:3), the fourth spans a whole octave of two to four since (2 times 3) : (3 times 4) simplifies to 1:2.

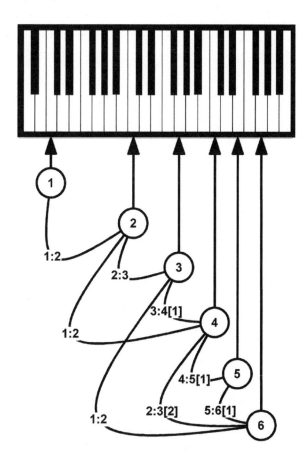

Figure 2.2. The musical ratios implicit in the first six numbers.

Five is the addition of two and three but it cannot be divided by them and so is a prime number. It introduces for the first time a relationship (4:5) called a major third in musical harmony. We will look into the *structure* of musical harmony shortly, but with the major third the start of musical expression becomes possible. The octave is being steadily populated internally, creating more internal structure within itself. Through these internal notes, musical melody and harmony become possible.

After five, and for the first time, the numbers two and three come together in six which is the product of two times three. This forms another octave, but this time to three, as 3:6 is the proportion 1:2. A new minor third destined to make us somber is formed with five, as the ratio 5:6. The new major and minor thirds can be seen to divide up the perfect fifth.

This property of later musical ratios to subdivide earlier ratios, in pairs, is true throughout the number field (fig. 2.3). The thirds them-

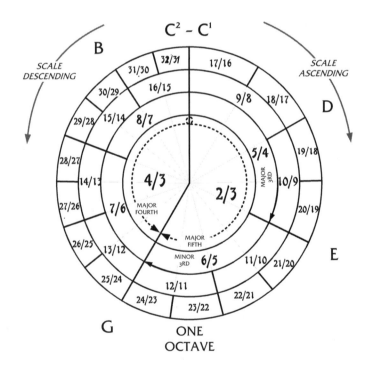

Figure 2.3. The Wheel of Generation in which later ratios fill earlier ones, the wheel being logarithmic where the full circle represents an octave doubling.

selves are subdivided by ratios created by the proximity of the numbers eight, nine, and ten and then ten, eleven, and twelve. John Michell has suggested that it was just these first twelve numbers that the ancients identified as being the primary gods of the creation.

The next octave, between six and twelve, is the creator of two whole tones called major (8:9) and minor (9:10) (fig. 2.4). The modern keyboard is not tuned to show the difference between these because the ubiquitous even-tempered scale used today adopts a constant ratio for the semitone, a logarithmic twelfth of the octave. Each of the twelve semitones is given an irrational proportion (1.0595), the twelfth root of two (1:2), forcing all whole tones to be twice this ratio, always the same, and never a pure tone of either 8:9 or 9:10.

There are also two new prime numbers between six and twelve,

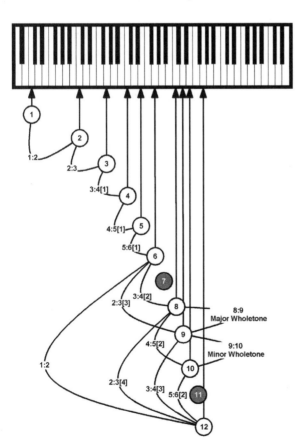

Figure 2.4. The harmonic ratios created by the number range up to twelve.

namely seven and eleven. These numbers have very important uses in ancient metrology, not least because they figure in the best simple approximation to pi (the perimeter length of a circle when the diameter is one) as 22/7. But in the world of harmony seven and eleven appear to be bypassed, as in figure 2.4, since *by definition*[1] harmony itself is based on ratios involving only two, three, and five. Seven and eleven can have their own musical ratios but these are avoided in most conventional music and they fall outside normal musical harmony. For instance, seven leads to the septenary third (6:7), which is "more minor" than the minor third of 5:6, and also to the septenary whole tone (7:8) which is "more major" than the major whole tone of 8:9.

Thus seven forms a gulf of lesser harmony until 6:8 produces 3:4, a perfect fourth, to arrive at the realm of the whole tones, 8:9 and 9:10. The prime eleven then creates another disharmony in the developing system, which is bridged by the minor third (5:6) to reach twelve.

A very important principle emerges within the field of number as it evolves what is, to us, harmony. As stated, the prime numbers two, three, and five are responsible for the principle of harmony; this means that all the higher primes are fated to occupy the voids left by the field of harmony.

However, the primes seven and eleven form part of the primary creation too. As we will see in the next chapter, the ratio between Earth's mean radius and its meridian is 22/7 (two times 11/7). These numbers therefore have a very special place in the system of the ancients. As we will see, they were preferred and employed as essential to *the relationship between linear and rotational measure*. The ancients used 22/7 as pi,* which enabled them to avoid its irrational nature and rooted their ideal with the two primes less than twelve but not employed in harmony. This maximized the rationality and simplicity of their work.

Figure 2.5 abandons the keyboard view and adopts a circular geometry to show all the harmonies occurring between one and twenty-four.

---

*The difference between 22/7 and pi is that it is 0.001265 larger, an accuracy of 99.96%.

The only new harmonic ratio that emerges is that of the half tone 15:16. The "voids" between the established harmonic intervals are filled by the next primes, thirteen, seventeen, nineteen, and twenty-three, plus numbers that, while not primes, are products of the "earlier" non-harmonic primes within the 6:12 octave: seven and eleven.

The half tone 15:16 arises after a leading major third of 4:5 (16:20) and the two tones together then complete the perfect fourth, 3:4 (12:16). This new way of dividing the perfect fourth holds the key to modal music, as we shall see. The prime thirteen, within this interval, is accompanied by the doubling of seven, fourteen. The primes seventeen and nineteen have popped into the gaps within the two types of whole tone. Finally, multiples of seven and then eleven (twenty-one and twenty-two)

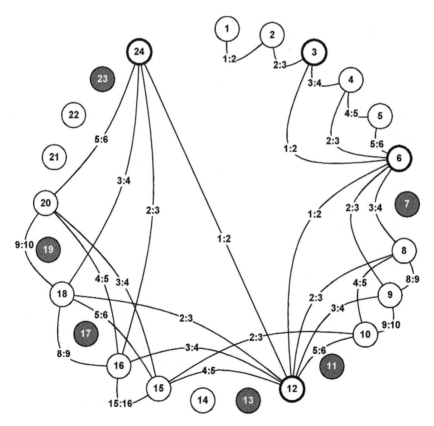

Figure 2.5. The first twenty-four numbers and their harmonic interplay building the world of harmony itself.

precede the prime twenty-three within the completing interval of the minor third or 5:6.

This may at first seem to be simply a result of the rules of multiplication, but in fact it is a demonstration that the field of number is the source of harmony. Any number that does not fit within "the system" by definition does not contain two, three, and five. The later prime numbers obviously fit this description. Harmony is therefore "created" by the numbers two, three, and five. One can guarantee that wherever a perfect interval exists between two vibrations *or two measurements,* then the whole numbers two, three, and five must be employed to fulfill the sequences 1:2:3:4:5:6 and 8:9:10 and 15:16!

What is surprising in this octave 12:24 is that, although musical *articulation* is very restricted within it, much harmony has basically arisen from "just" the field of number, within just the first twenty-four numbers. Also astonishing is that the new primes crop up *naturally* within the harmonic voids, along with the products of earlier voids. In this sense, the number field was probably seen as a primordial building in itself.

The science of metrology is similarly structured to find the units that maintain simplicity of relationship between different dimensions of built or implied circles. The way to transmit such knowledge and hence to learn about it, was therefore through the building and study of monuments and landscape temples built according to it.

OF MODES AND MEASURES

To complete the journey into recognizable musical octaves, the territory between twenty-four and forty-eight creates a series of harmonies corresponding to one of the Greek modes (fig. 2.6). We would call this the Ionian mode because the *scale* starts off with two tones and a semitone. If a scale is started at a larger number, the other modes such as the Dorian mode can be built, in that case between twenty-seven and fifty-four, using the same intermediate number "nodes."

At this point though, the discussion needs to focus on the impact

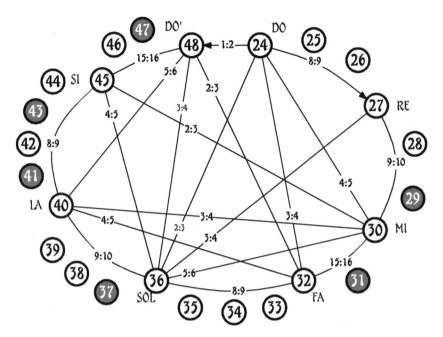

Figure 2.6. *The octave twenty-four to forty-eight that introduces the possibility of modal music based upon the sequencing of tones and semitones within the octave.*

of these ideas of harmony and number on the ancient model of Earth that became its *metrological application*. If two, three, and five are "the gods" of the numerical world, and the larger primes are "the demons," then traditionally there is a tug of war between them in the essential process of world creation. The no man's land in between appears to be the two primes seven and eleven, occurring before the number twelve, thought to be the "limit of the divine world."

Extending harmonic relation to allow the septenary tones such as 7/6 and 8/7 corresponds to actual units of measurement in the ancient world, known as the "Russian foot" and "royal (Egyptian) foot" respectively. When eleven is permitted in ratios and proportions, then 11/10 and 12/11 can be recognized as the "Saxon" and "Sumerian feet." These measures are pure fractions of what is today termed an "English foot," which was taken to be unity within a system of measures developed from these ideas of proportional harmony, a system apparently global in application. Even though the ancient measures were all a part of a single unified system, they have been rediscovered separately, so each type of foot has been named in accordance with the place where it was first identified. (Please refer to appendix 2 for further elaboration.)

MEASURE	FRACTION	DECIMAL
Russian	7/6	1.166666
Royal	8/7	1.142857
Saxon	11/10	1.1
Sumerian	12/11	1.090909
English	1/1	1.0

In these ratios, all the adjacencies in the range one to twelve are being recognized as significant. The ratios involving seven are intervals recognized in some types of music such as Balinese gamelan, and other ethnic and experimental music.

Beyond twelve, there is a companion to the half tone of 16/15 in 15/14 that exists in metrological form as the root Belgic foot. There is also a type of quarter note below twenty-four in the Persian foot ratio of 21/20 feet.

Figure 2.7 illustrates what happens when seven and eleven ratios take part in a harmonic creation. A new semitone arrives as 14:15 (aka 15/14); a further fifth of 2:3 arrives at twenty-one and the quarter tone, found in gamelan music, of 20:21 (aka 21/20, the Persian foot). The other quarter tone defined by just two, three, and five is 24:25; 24/25 is the root value for the Roman foot (0.96 ft).

Ignoring the higher prime of twenty-three, there are five interesting numbers in the region of the quarter tone, namely twenty, twenty-one, twenty-two, then twenty-four and twenty-five. On either side are the primes nineteen and twenty-six (2 times 13) and twenty-three within; these are the full range of available quarter tone generating numbers using only such small numbers.

The work on ancient metrology undertaken by John Neal and John Michell has revealed that the ancients did not just define types of foot in harmonic proportion to the English foot, but also varied these feet by

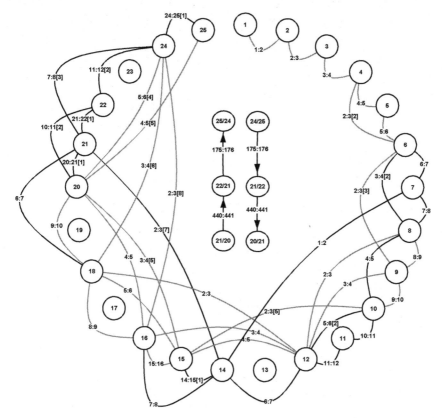

Figure 2.7. Adding the harmonic relations involving seven and eleven to find their creative powers below twenty-five.

two ratios: 441/440 and 176/175. These ratios both incorporate seven and eleven since their formulae are:

$$441/440 = (3^2 \times 7^2)/(2^3 \times 5 \times 11) = 1.002\overline{72}$$

$$176/175 = (2^4 \times 11)/(5^2 \times 7) = 1.00\overline{571428}$$

These ratios, along with their reciprocals and products, form a grid (see appendix 2 for the essential details).

Working out why the foot measurements were varied by these ratios is a challenge. However, we do know that the lengths of key degrees of latitude vary according to these ratios, specifically latitudes 10°, 31°,

51°, and 66°. Also, as we will see in the next chapter, the ratio of Earth's mean to polar radius is 441/440.

Two more factors are relevant when considering these ratios.

1. The two grid ratios are themselves the imperfect cancellation of the two different approximate values of 2 × pi (which calculates the circumference from the radius or half diameter):

$$441/440 = 63/10 \times 7/44$$
$$\text{and } 176/175 = 4/25 \times 44/7$$

2. Most significantly with regard to the ratios 21/20 and 25/24, the grid ratios can be decomposed once more as:

$$441/440 = 21/20 \times 21/22$$
$$\text{and } 176/175 = 24/25 \times 22/21$$

To summarize, there is a relationship between:

- the grid used to vary ancient measures,
- the approximations to pi used by the ancient world, and
- the ratios found at the end of the series one to twenty-five, where the primes two, three, five, seven, and eleven are considered harmonically generative.

Most importantly, the values of these grid constants point to the lengths of specific degrees on Earth's meridian, an imaginary line on the surface from the North Pole to the South Pole, which is elliptical in shape. What they reveal is that *the shape of Earth is related to the harmonic products of the first twenty-five numbers,* seen from the perspective of harmony, and employing only those prime numbers below twelve.

An ellipse, being a rotational function, has to involve pi, the rotational constant. However, by combining a mixture of the simplest approximations to pi—from three, through 63/10 and 25/4, to 22/7 (the most accurate)—the irrational form of pi and the ellipse are both avoided in the *numero-logical scheme* that provided the ancient model of Earth.

This is illustrated in figure 2.8 where the ratios involving twenty,

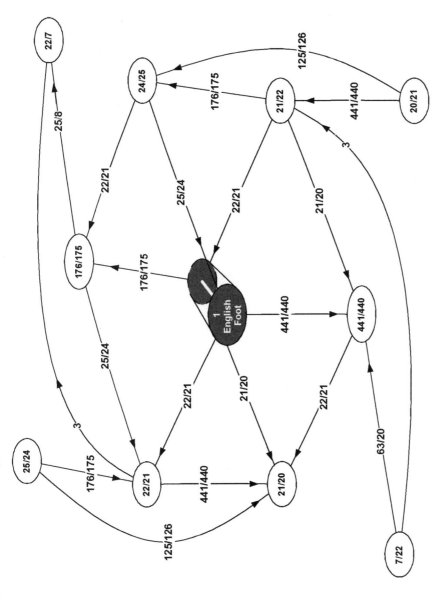

Figure 2.8. The relation of Neal and Michell's Grid Constants defining the shape of Earth using ratios of twenty, twenty-one, twenty-two, twenty-four, and twenty-five, metrological grid ratios 175:176 and 440:441 (see figure 3.1 and associated text), and the rational approximations to pi: three, 63/20, 25/8, and 22/7.

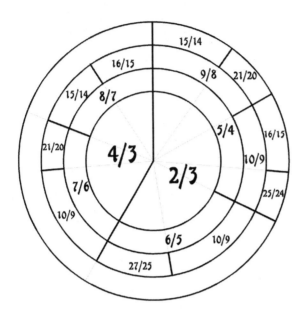

Figure 2.9. The Wheel
of Generation (figure
2.3) can be contained
using only semitones and
quarter notes, once the
prime seven is employed
within the ratios.

twenty-one, twenty-two, twenty-four, and twenty-five are integrated
with rational values of pi and the two grid constants.

Figure 2.9 shows how quarter tones and half tones can be used
to "cap" the division of tones by the higher primes. Another pseudo
half tone, 27/25, is required, which in metrology can be identified as
a Drusian foot! In this manner, the infinite growth of harmonic ratios
shown in figure 2.3 has been "capped" by half tones and quarter notes
that only employ two, three, five, and seven.

THREE

THE MODEL OF EARTH

The units of measurement in the ancient science of metrology specifically relate to the size and shape of Earth. Metrology began with the derivation of what we now call the English foot from the equatorial circumference, as well as from the recognition that the mean Earth radius can be perfectly expressed as $12^6 \times 7$ feet. This model is almost identical to the international models used today for the navigation and mapping of the planet. However, modern science measures things as found and not within a created scheme or order, which was the ancient approach.

This system today would be called a *model of reality*. Such a model has validity as either a *plan* from which something is built or an *approximation* to something real, which can be used as a proxy for the real thing, within calculations. From the standpoint of *numerical creationism,* the ancients might have viewed their model of Earth as the *actual plan* according to which Earth's rotation and hence ellipticity were organized, or it could have represented *their discovery of order* in the shape of the planet, itself an astounding revision of their supposed capabilities and interests. The main point is that this ancient model,[1] employing rigorous ideas of numerical harmony, indicates a need to model the shape of Earth.

THE MEAN AND PI

A true model of Earth needs to express the amount of polar flattening caused in the actual Earth by its rotation. Mean Earth dimensions
express Earth's size as it would be if it had not been deformed by its
rotation. Both the mean Earth circumference and radius (the distance
from its center to its circumference at the equator) have significant relations to the polar radius (the distance from Earth's center to either pole)
(fig. 3.1). For the mean circumference, this involves another approximation to pi, namely 63/10 or 6.3 (that is, pi = 3.15). While 63/10 is
not a very accurate pi, the consequence of 63/10 is that if the polar
radius is ten units long, then the mean circumference is sixty-three
units long. This is a very simple yet surprisingly accurate relationship,
one that enables the model to be easily remembered and simple calculations to be performed. This simplicity also makes it easy to use
in monumental representations of Earth, as indeed it was in ancient
monuments and landscape temples.

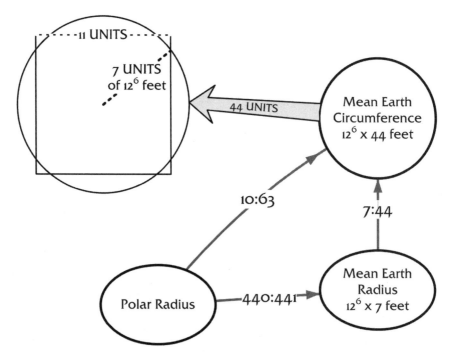

Figure 3.1. The simple inner relations between the polar radius and mean Earth.

It is the polar to mean radius, however, that yields the key parameter in the shape of Earth, for if the polar radius is divided by 440 then the unit created, multiplied by 441, generates the mean radius. This fact, discovered by John Michell, unlocks the ancient model of Earth.

The key relation, 440:441, originates from the operation of numerical harmony. The last chapter demonstrated that within the first twenty-four numbers, the ratio 441/440 can be found between two ratios, 21/20 and 21/22.* When multiplied, these two ratios produce 441, which is 21^2, and 440, which is 22 times 20. Thus, while the ratio 441/440 looks like an obscure ratio formed from large numbers, it is in fact a direct product of the first twenty-four numbers. The division of the polar radius by 440, multiplied by 21/20, produces a length of 21 × 22. This multiplied by 21/22 creates 21^2 or 441. This ratio between twenty-two (2 × 11) and twenty-one (3 × 7) is completely related to 22/7.

In this ancient model the mean Earth radius divides by seven, leaving a unit of 12^6 feet. Remembering that 22/7 is the simplest accurate approximation to pi, and noting that a radius is half the diameter, then the circumference of the mean Earth is 12^6 × 44 feet around. This is the same as the perimeter of a square with side eleven times 12^6 feet long.

The mean Earth was considered symbolically as being the essence of Earth, and as such it is also portrayed as the four-gated square city. Square mandalas, the City of Zion, Jerusalem, and other square structures represent the round Earth as a square material *building*. Circular representations relate instead to eternity for ideas about *eternity* emerge from the nature of planetary cycles of orbit and rotation, which repeat *endlessly*.

It is to be expected that such ideas should have been represented as gods by cultures that found numbers to be *demonstrably creative*, as the

---

*In the developing world of number, twenty-one and twenty-two are the *first adjacency* of seven and eleven (the primes not primary to the system of harmony); such "adjacency" is a principle found in the world of super-particular fractions that so shapes the emergence of harmonic ideas. Super-particular fractions are made up of a denominator and numerator that are only one apart and are of the form n : n + 1 where n is any number, for example, 3/2 or 5/4.

gods are, *by definition*. The god of measure in Egypt was Thoth and his iconography expresses the act of measurement, his nose being a writing implement and his arms spanning the sector of a circle (fig. 3.2). Thoth's arms are "fathoming" one edge of a hexagon between his thumbs, which are twenty-one of the implicit grid lengths apart. This makes the radius of a circle containing the hexagon twenty-one units too, and then, using pi as 22/7, the circumference is 2 × 21 × 22/7; the sevens cancel to yield a circumference of 132 (6 × 22). Thus the sector above Thoth's fathom of twenty-one is twenty-two long, so that *he himself is* the rational approximation of pi. This ratio of 21/22 and its reciprocal—which I call the Thoth ratio—are implicit in the ratio 441/440 of mean and polar radii. In this way Thoth perfectly represents ancient concerns relating to measure, the shape of Earth, and the rationalization of pi to connect with the numerical root of creation itself.

It is worth noting also that Thoth's iconography contains the concept of twelve-foldness in the sense that the angles generated are based on thirty degree steps that divide into the whole 360 degree circle as

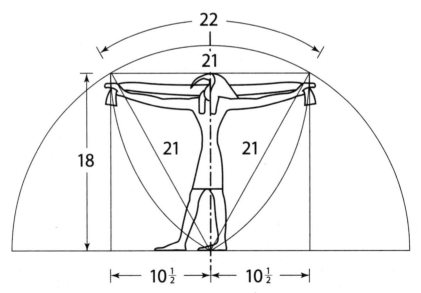

Figure 3.2. The iconography of Thoth as directly relating to the sector of a circle and the ratio twenty-two to twenty-one. (Drawing from R. A. Schwaller de Lubicz, The Temple of Man [Rochester, Vt.: Inner Traditions, 1998].)

twelve sectors. In this way the divine world is represented as the zodiac of twelve, even though such ideas appear to emerge only later with the evolution of a solar godhead.

A famous formula connects the Golden Mean (φ), the minor third (6/5), and pi (π), namely $\varphi^2 \times 6/5 = \pi$ where $\pi = 3.1416408$, which gives a very accurate pi, accurate to 0.00153 of a percent. As pi is the perimeter length of a circle when the diameter is one, if the diameter is the Golden Mean squared or φ^2, then the perimeter is $6\varphi^2/5$ (8.2247).

The Golden Mean was considered a fundamental constant by the Egyptians and *the* fundamental division of the whole into two parts. The six parts of the circumference are exactly the hexagon of Thoth, half of which is shown in the figure. Using 22/7 as π reveals a practical result of

$$\varphi^2 = (22 \times 5) / (7 \times 6) = 55/21 = 2.6190476$$

In this the Thoth ratio of 22/21 is simply $\pi/3$. That makes $\pi = 22/7$ a yard of feet with the length of 22/21, which is 440/441 of the Persian foot (21/20 feet). This indicates how the metrological system is a complete system, integral with the ancient model of Earth and, as we shall see, with prehistoric monuments depicting that model.

THE SEARCH FOR THE FOOT THAT FITS

While the number of feet in the mean Earth radius has been mentioned, how such a foot was arrived at is a question begged until now. To understand how this crucial step was taken in metrology, it is important to see that *ratios are unitless* and that they only refer to abstract proportions.

In contrast, when we consider what is divided, for example the polar radius, 1/440 part of it is an actual length. That is a unit of measure that might then be regarded as "cosmic," since it also divides into the mean Earth radius 441 times. In practice, a unit related to the human scale was required, hence the name foot, but how was it derived?

The English foot can in fact be derived from the equator *as well as* the mean Earth radius. Based upon Earth itself, this foot became the base unit one for the whole system of measure that was derived from it. That system included:

- a set of harmonically related "root" feet that were simple ratios of the base foot and
- geodetically valid variations of these feet as "modules."[2]

The rotation of Earth "cuts up" the solar year, which is its orbital period, 365.242 times in units of days. If the equator is divided into 365.242 pieces, which could be called "angular days" (being in fact the angle traveled by the Sun in one day), then a unit of length is again measurable. The English foot was taken to be 1/1000 of 1/360 of a day's angle on the equator (and not a fraction of a degree of longitude).

The division by 360 is there for two reasons: It enables degrees of *latitude* to be measured so as to yield a number of feet that resemble the year numerically; and it converts the north–south meridian into 360 measurable units called degrees. Three hundred and sixty is made of just two, three, and five, as its formula is $2^3 \times 3^2 \times 5$, and so 360 is a harmonic number that was introduced into the definition of the foot to remove the non-harmonic 365 or 365.242 days in the solar year. In similar fashion, the day is split up into twenty-four hours, the sky into the same number of hours of "right ascension" (referring to Earth rotational time relative to the spring equinoctal point) and the equator into 360 degrees of longitude, all to introduce harmonic rationality.

Simultaneously, the mean Earth radius is $12^6 \times 7$ of the same foot measurement in the ancient model.[3] The foot thus represents a masterful solution to the problem of finding the *perfect ruler,* in the sense of a *metrological root* for Earth's design and also therefore a *god-ruler of creation* itself and its plan. If the day length is measured upon the Equator, then the first task is to see how *time translates into length* at the equator. This gives the necessary objectivity to a unit of length intended to relate the celestial sphere to Earth.

A foot that had not been derived from a cosmic dimension would have been arbitrary and rootless. Once established in this way, however, the foot related every monument built using it to the cosmic and made the building process a recapitulation of the cosmic act.

DERIVING AN ACCURATE MODEL

Two skills were prerequisite in the derivation of the ancient model of Earth:

1. the ability to measure a long section of Earth's surface, between two accurately measured points in time and space;
2. the understanding of the geometry of the ellipse, found in planetary orbits, and that of the naturally deformed spheres of the spinning planets.

The first skill is called surveying and involves accurate star measurements and accurate Earth measurements, the very same techniques as those used to map the world in more recent times. The knowledge of one length upon Earth to high accuracy can be extended by finding the bearing, from each of its ends, to a third point—hence the name *triangulation* for this technique. Britain, for example, was triangulated over its mainland length in modern times, without any re-measurement of an actual length. The result was surprisingly accurate, providing each angle was measured repeatedly to ensure an accurate average.

The measuring of star angles in the sky is effectively the same technology. The surveying of the equator, of the north–south meridian degrees, and of the angles between celestial objects all involve the measurement of angles "on Earth as it is in Heaven."

The development of sacred geometry (as one of the traditional arts) naturally emerged from solving geodetic problems, as did the ability to comprehend the ellipse as a practical manifestation of the circle in nature. In the ancient model:

- The ratio of pole to mean radii creates an ellipse in which the great circle of the north–south meridian is close in length to the mean Earth circumference.
- The equator has a radius at a right angle to the Pole, and its circumference is used to define the length of the foot, as a unit that divides into the circumference (as the product of the solar year in days times 360,000), *while also* dividing into the mean radius as $12^6 \times 7$.

In other words, *the foot is the solution to a simultaneous equation* of both deformation and mean size. Combined with the pole to mean ratio, the derivation of the foot, at a stroke, defines Earth in a manner that takes into account the reality of celestial time, the shape of Earth, its mean size, and the development of harmony from the earliest numbers. Having evolved a paradigm of the universe as a numerical creation by counting celestial time periods, the ancients then further elaborated their worldview by finding suitable units for "the gods'" plan for the creation of Earth, using the miraculous simplicity of numerical relationships.

It is important that the foot is commensurate simultaneously with the key dimensions of Earth because it then becomes available for calculations involving both the Pole and the meridian circumference. The meridian is $12^6 \times 44$ feet in the model; eleven can be removed from it by using a measure with units of eleven feet within its formula. The English mile is 5,280 feet long and has the formula $2^5 \times 3 \times 5 \times 11 = 5280$. When the ideal meridian is divided by the mile to measure it in miles, the eleven in the mile's formula cancels the eleven in the forty-four of $12^6 \times 44$ feet. The result is, as stated by Michell, $12^5/10$ or 24,883.2 miles long.

Any meridian measure in feet therefore requires a formula (X/Y) times eleven, where X and Y are within the range of numbers only made up of two, three, and five. That is, a meridian measure has within its "prefix" the (X/Y), the harmonic primes two, three, and five, with a further eleven in the numerator. The Saxon Foot of 11/10 is one such measure, leading to a meridian length of $12^6 \times 40$ Saxon feet.

As mentioned earlier, this meridian can be divided by sixty-three and multiplied by ten to give, by one route, the length of the Pole. This procedure will not remove the eleven in the numerator and secondly it will add a seven into the denominator of the polar radius length. Therefore, the formula for a polar unit of length, in feet, has to be (X/Y), the harmonic component, times (11/7), the part made up of those primes below twelve yet above six (in contrast to the harmonic component that consists of the primes below six).

To generate a polar measure first requires that the seven be removed from the polar radius, otherwise there will be a repeating fraction produced by 1/7.*

Secondly, the eleven in the numerator could be removed, but the only consequence of not doing so will be that the result will be a number involving eleven, a non-harmonic prime. In fact the best polar measures always have (11/7) in their formula in feet.

The most famous polar measure is the *sacred cubit* associated with the Jews and their Temple of Solomon. The longer sacred cubit is ($2^8 \times 3^4/5^6$) times (11/7) = 2.08544914 feet. The Pole measured in these terms is then 10 million sacred cubits; from this it can also be seen that in the ancient model the meridian must be 63/10 of this or 63 million sacred cubits. This knowledge was current in the community of Portuguese sailors, as noted by Edward Wright:

> And albeit the Globe of the earth and water, compared with the sphaeres of the starres, is as it were a center or prick; yet being considered by itself, it containeth in the greatest circle 6300 common Spanish leagues.[4]

Dividing 63 million by 6,300 yields 10,000 sacred cubits as a Spanish league, maintaining the 10:63 ratio, Pole to meridian, using a polar measure—the sacred cubit.

This cubit was sought by Isaac Newton, who needed to know the shape of Earth's elliptical profile in order to estimate the mass of Earth

---

*Seven being that number most incompatible with the other numbers below ten, a fact noted well and often in the ancient world.

and test his theory of gravitation, through a calculation of the Moon's orbit. The length of the equator was known by him to sufficient accuracy, giving him the major axis of the ellipse. The Pole could not be easily measured but it was rumored to be implicit in the ancient unit of the sacred cubit and to be found in the monuments of Egypt.* He sent his friend John Greaves to study the Great Pyramid; though much of value derived from this, in the end Newton had to use a French meridian degree measurement to estimate the profile of the meridian.

The existence of such traditional knowledge and units of measure indicates that the ancients already knew the polar radius. In the past, some group must have measured the lengthening of the meridian degrees on the meridian; from this the shape of Earth had been extrapolated as an ellipse, and the ancient model developed from it. Any culture capable of global navigation or wishing to measure Earth for any other reason, would have done the same that our modern culture has again done. The ancients, however, also placed the basic parameters of their model into a framework based upon their theory of harmony and the numbers below twelve.

The polar measure relative to the foot is perfectly portrayed in one of the themes of the Great Pyramid, namely its height of seven units (representing the Pole) and its base of eleven units (representing the meridian).

The following table shows the defined elements of the model and the sort of dimensions found in the scientific age[5] as I have presented them, all in miles of 5,280 feet.

If we divided the modern equatorial circumference by 360,000 we would obtain 365.2223 rather than 365.242. This means that the ancient model had arrived at a very close figure to the solar year in days, which would have been a natural cue to deriving the foot from the equator through the year number and 360,000. It would be an enormous coincidence that the equator divides by the solar year to give 360,000 feet.

The rest of the ancient model gives remarkably accurate results by sticking to similar "purist" principles, namely the use of rational approximations to pi. The net effect is to provide a very simple numeri-

---

*Surviving texts said it was the 10 millionth part of the Pole in length.

DIMENSION	ANCIENT	MODERN	DIFFERENCE	ACCURACY
Equatorial Radius	3,963.414	3,963.207	–0.207	99.995%
Equatorial Circumference	24,902.864	24,901.566	–1.298	99.995%
Mean Radius	3,958.691	3,958.775	0.084	99.998%
Mean Circumference	24,883.200	24,873.714	–9.486	99.962%
Meridian Circumference	24,883.200	24,859.868	–23.332	99.906%
Polar Radius	3,949.714	3,949.919	0.205	99.995%

cal framework, easy to remember and transmit, with virtually no loss of accuracy and considerable symbolic consistency to this day. The pole divides by the sacred number seven and the mean Earth meridian naturally has eleven as its highest prime number.

The Pole and the mean became the core of an ancient monumental symbolism employing appropriately structured ancient measures rational to the foot. The Pole, for example, is 288 times 1,152 times 440 times 1/7 feet long. This makes certain numbers available, using different units, to model the Pole within a monument. This is achieved by the combination of units used in a monument and the resulting scaling of a monument to the Pole. We will see in the next chapter that the Great Pyramid uses the 440/441 numbers in height and that geodetically aligned triangles discovered in Britain, laid out on the landscape, throw up the numbers 288 and 1152.

Much of the surviving monumentalism within the ancient world appears to derive from a common system of measurement based on a simple numerical model of the shape of Earth. One function of ancient monuments has been to allow such information to travel through time. This information can be recovered through studying the monuments built using it. It will become obvious in the next chapter that such reference lengths as the "royal mile" or Sumerian foot are always built into monuments as clues where they embody a ratio between the monument and reference lengths within the ancient model of Earth.

FOUR

ANCIENT THEME PARKS

The ancient model described in chapter 3 leaves us with five key lengths, all having numerical components that contain the prime numbers two, three, five, seven, and eleven, when expressed in English feet. These are the lengths of:

- the polar radius
- the mean radius
- the equatorial radius
- the circumference of the mean Earth
- the circumference at the equator

Ancient monument builders, almost without exception, encoded the relationships between two or more of these dimensions of Earth within the dimensions of a monument.

Megalithic examples are found in the Great Pyramid, the lost Temple of Solomon, a number of British landscape triangles that relate to Stonehenge, and the dimensions found within Stonehenge itself. It is very difficult to conceive that this widespread occurrence of the same ratios and metrological system could be an accidental property of megalithic building.

Furthermore, this circumstance continues on through the Iron Age brochs (round tower-like dry stone structures in Scotland), Greek temples, and then medieval buildings such as the Gothic cathedrals, except that the *size of Earth* was no longer the focus. Instead metrology was used within a new tradition of sacred geometry in which the result was symbolic and totemic rather than cosmically objective. However, in the last three hundred years there are examples of metrological constructions employing this new tradition secretly, notably in Washington, D.C. (see chapter 10).

In other words, the legacy of Atlantis, that is, of Atlantean knowledge, is visible through the study of monumental building through the ages. In this chapter, some analysis involving well-known exemplar monuments is provided to demonstrate exactly how this knowledge was employed in practice.

AN INTRODUCTION TO SQUARES AND CIRCLES

There are two important ways in which squares and circles can interact. The first is to enclose one within the other and the second is to draw both with the same perimeter length (see fig. 4.1). A square can enclose a circle, touching only at the middle of the square's sides, or a circle can enclose a square, in which case the corners of the square touch the circle. When a square and circle have the same perimeter length their relationship is described as "squaring the circle."

Construction of a square that "squares the circle" became a sign of geometric wisdom. We shall see that it is the operator pi that effectively governs such a relationship, as pi is the cosmic constant of translation between linear ("in a line") dimensions and radial ("rotating about a point") or *angular* measure. The issue behind such sacred geometrical facts is that the eternal world appears as orbit and rotation, in contrast to life within Earth's space that operates in linear measure. These two types of measure are extensive and intensive: linear measure extends a dimension, while angular measure divides the whole that already exists,

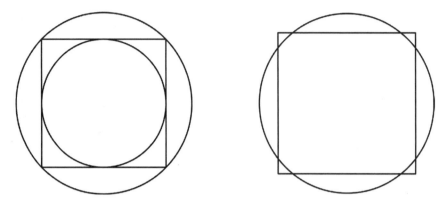

Figure 4.1. Two important ways circles and squares interact in sacred geometry. Left: A circle can inscribe a square or a square inscribe a circle. Right: A square can also have the same perimeter length to "square the circle."

making the whole more intense or meaningful. In this way, the meaning of circle and square within the mind of the sacred geometer quite probably come with all the baggage of eternity versus existence—a dualism that offers a path of knowing through the study of geometric behavior.

If a circle of diameter one is inscribed within a square, then the square will have a perimeter length of four, while the circle will have a circumference of pi (fig. 4.2).

The difference between four and pi is easier to see using the anciently favored approximation to pi of 22/7 ($3.\overline{142857}$ is 99.96% accurate).

$$4 - 22/7 = (28 - 22)/7 = 6/7.$$

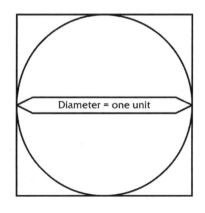

Diameter = one unit

Figure 4.2. An inscribed circle of unit length.

Figure 4.3. The difference between the perimeters of the circle and the square can be expressed as a circle with a diameter that is 3/11 of the larger circle's diameter. The Moon is exactly in this proportion to the mean Earth.

This difference in perimeter can be expressed as a circle with a diameter 6/7 times 7/22. The sevens cancel to leave 6/22 as its diameter, which simplifies to 3/11 of the original, inscribed circle (fig. 4.3).

This ratio of 3:11 is exactly the ratio between the Moon's diameter (1,080 miles) and the diameter of the mean Earth (the first major treatment of this was in *City of Revelation* by John Michell, who was responsible for its rediscovery[1]). From this we can see that the Moon represents the difference between an inscribed circle and the square that encloses it, by having a circumference that is the difference between the perimeters of the inscribed circle and enclosing square.

The baggage associated with this simple but cosmic geometrical fact is that Earth represents a sphere of materiality, and things material are symbolized as being square. The Moon is therefore, symbolically, that which materializes Earth from an eternal circular form into a place. Whether or not one wishes to enter into such a symbolic meaning, the bare fact that the Moon, originally projected from Earth, came to possess just this pi dimensional relationship implies there were extraordinary influences at work in its creation.

Placing this 3/11 Moon circle so that it just touches the mean Earth, it can be rolled around the greater circle in what was called the "sublunar orbit." This orbit demonstrates the second relationship of square to circle called "squaring the circle." The circle created by the center of the

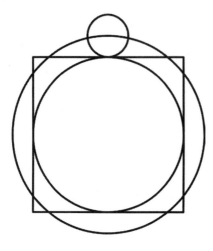

Figure 4.4. The center of the Moon describes a circle with the same perimeter as the square inscribed by the mean Earth.

Moon as it is rolled around Earth has the same perimeter as the square that encloses the mean Earth. Figure 4.4 only contains three perimeters, those of Earth and the Moon and that of their combined circumference, equal to the enclosing square. If the diameter of the Moon is re-scaled to consist of just three units, then the diameter of the mean Earth, in the same units, must be eleven units long. Between the centers, the distance between Earth and the Moon is then 11/2 plus 3/2 which equals 14/2 or just seven units.

THE PYRAMID, PI, AND THE MOON

This ratio between the diameter of the mean Earth as eleven and the distance between the centers of Earth and the Moon as seven is the exact ratio built into the Great Pyramid of Giza (fig. 4.5). Eleven over seven is the relationship of a radius to a quarter sector of a circle, and in the case of Earth, a quarter sector is symbolic of the distance between the Pole and the equator.

The Pyramid, according to Neal and Michell, was built to have an uncapped height of 1/11 of a mile.* In figure 4.6 this is equated with Earth's polar radius. Since a mile is 5,280 or $2^5 \times 3 \times 5 \times 11$ feet, then

---

*480 feet is 1/11 of 5,280 miles.

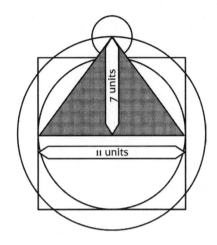

Figure 4.5. The Great Pyramid of Giza
has the exact shape to demonstrate the
3:11 relationship of the Moon to Earth
(after John Michell).

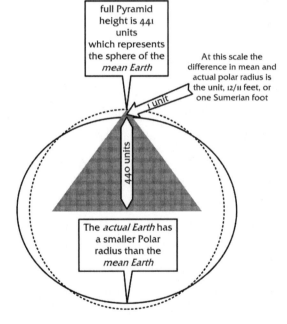

Figure 4.6. The use of units
to define polar and mean
Earth radii in the uncapped
and full height of the Great
Pyramid.

dividing by eleven yields 480 feet ($2^5 \times 3 \times 5$). The ancient model gives a
ratio of 440:441 for the pole to mean radii. Dividing 480 ($4 \times 12 \times 10$)
by 440 ($4 \times 11 \times 10$) gives the basic unit for the Pyramid's construction
as being just 12/11 feet, a type of foot now called the Sumerian foot.
There must be 440 such feet (1/11 mile) without the cap and 441 such

feet once the full height is realized by adding just one more Sumerian foot of 12/11 feet equal to $1.\overline{09}$ feet.

However, the simplest unit for measuring the Pole itself is undoubtedly the "royal mile," which is a mile of feet that are 8/7 feet long. This foot, called the "royal foot," was heavily employed within Egypt, turning up in the root form of the "sacred cubit" of 12/7 feet, a cubit of one and a half rather than of two feet. The polar radius measured in royal miles is 3,456 royal miles in length.

The scale of the Great Pyramid, with respect to its height and the ancient model of Earth, can then be calculated, via pole or mean. The scaling chosen makes five feet in the monument equivalent to thirty-six royal miles—7.2 royal miles per English foot.*

Using the mean Earth as $12^6 \times 7$ feet in the ancient model, then dividing by 441 ($3^2 \times 7^2$) leaves $2^{12} \times 3^4/7$ or 47,396.571 feet of the polar radius per Sumerian foot. The seven can be removed by dividing by the 8/7 royal foot, and the "per Sumerian foot" unit can be converted by multiplying it out as 12/11, to leave again 7.2 royal miles per foot. The mile, by containing eleven in its formula ($2^5 \times 3 \times 5 \times 11$), and the royal foot, containing seven (8/7), creates this perfect polar unit, the royal mile, that has 11/7 implicit relative to the English foot on which the ancient model of Earth was based.

In the simple diagram of the two circles of Earth and Moon (figure 4.5), the mean Earth was not shown as the Pyramid height but rather as its base. If the base is also a reference to the mean Earth then it would have a different scaling to Earth than the Pyramid's height model.

John Neal has shown that the Pyramid's side length was obscured by calculations based on taking an average of the four side lengths. This came from the misconception that they were designed to be identical in length and that the average would therefore give increased accuracy. However, the sides were of different lengths, with good reason, as Neal shows. The south side of the pyramid was built to be exactly 756 feet long, which is 441 sacred cubits of 12/7 feet. This compares with the

---

*3,456 royal miles divided by 7.2 royal miles yields 480 units.

height model scale of 441 feet of 12/11 feet, showing the ubiquitous relationship of seven and eleven within the structure.

However, we wish to divide the base not by seven but by eleven since the diagram had the mean Earth diameter as eleven units—but what are these units? New units can be evolved to translate something with seven in its formula to something with eleven in its formula, as does 22/7 as pi. The suitable ratio is the pole to mean ratio of 440:441. It was applied to the sacred cubit to make it longer so that the longer measure could then be applied to the monument to make the south side just 440 of the longer cubits. The unit is revealed by dividing by eleven to yield forty "standard sacred cubits" (SSC), as they are called by Neal. Seven times forty such cubits is 481.$\overline{09}$ feet, the assumed full height of the Great Pyramid. The two different models are related as 5.5:7 or 11:14, and this ratio emerges directly from the fact that:

- the mean Earth is the original circle within the 3:11 diagram
- the combined Moon-Earth radius defines the Pyramid ratio of 7:11
- the Pyramid has the ancient model of Pole to mean height encoded within its height.

The Egyptian builders then drop a further bombshell, revealed by Neal, that the height times the base length, in English feet, is the length of the degree of latitude for Giza at 30° North (fig. 4.7). This is best seen as the area, in square feet, of the rectangle that encloses the Pyramid of height seven and base eleven. In our common units of standard sacred cubits, the height is 280 and the base 440 and the result is 123,200 SSC, which does not give the degree length.

It is in the nature of such a rectangular calculation that the product involves its units as a square. Thus every different unit would give a differing *numerical result*; it is only when the English foot is employed that the Pyramid unlocks the required length for 30° latitude (29.5° to 30.5°) in those feet.

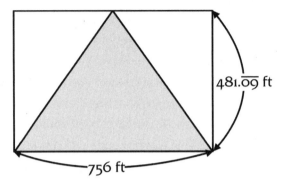

Figure 4.7. How the Great Pyramid encodes the degree of latitude (after John Neal). Each side of the pyramid is a different length and each length times the pyramid height gives (in square feet) the length of a different degree of latitude within Egypt in linear feet. The southern side is the exact number of feet to generate (in square feet) the number of feet between latitudes 29.5° and 30° north.

Height = 441 × 12/11 = 481.$\overline{09}$ = $2^2 \times 3^3 \times 7^2/11$ feet

Latitude (30°N) = 363704.$\overline{72}$ = $2^4 \times 3^6 \times 7^3/11$ feet

South Side = 756 = $2^2 \times 3^3 \times 7$ feet

∴ Scale of South Side (latitude divided by length of South Side) =

1°$_{30}$ / 756 = height of Pyramid

The implications come quick and fast, not least that the Egyptians had measured a degree of latitude accurately, confirming their knowledge of the triangulation technology required for such a task. Also confirmed is *the pre-eminent position of the English foot as one* in the system of other feet employed by ancient metrology.

The greatest truth revealed by this has to be that the scaling used for the twin models of Pyramid height and base length, relative to the ancient model of Earth, are defined by the requirement to create a rectangle that expresses the latitude of the monument. The Pyramid was defined by Earth (its polar and mean radii) and the English foot. (Perhaps this is why Newton's friend John Greaves, when visiting this Pyramid to measure its units, inscribed his English foot standard within the King's Chamber with the motto "To be observed by all nations.") It is then relatively obvious that the remaining three sides might define other degrees of latitude within Egypt by having shorter lengths than the south side, and this is found to be the case.

The Great Pyramid is therefore *far greater* than is generally realized. While its size has given it a stubborn tenacity in the face of vandals and natural forces alike, it stands in a field of utter simplicity when seen with eyes trained in the traditional arts. But its simplicity, even when revealed, is hard to communicate since its messages are multi-dimensional and require a grasp of the type of thinking involved.

It is remarkable that the Moon fulfills the size requirement to square Earth, and that the Pyramid speaks directly of this construction, then goes on to demonstrate its location upon Earth relative to the ancient model. But our modern culture will only be able to process this fact by changing important parts of itself, from a clumsy status quo where academics toil and tourists turn up. Having over-achieving ancestors could be a bit embarrassing for we would not know how to place them within the modern context. Most embarrassing is the fact that they were obviously onto something that we have little clue about today, and that they acted with an extraordinary sense of purpose to demonstrate, perhaps to us, that they were not practicing some empty religion but could prove that the world was built according to measure.

Symbolically, the location of the Pyramid at the base of the Nile Delta relates the delta to the iconography of Thoth (fig. 4.8). Piazzi Smyth provides this interesting observation, which then has direct relevance to the Pyramid's role within the project of measuring the degree of latitude within the delta itself. If the degree from 30–31° is the height of the Pyramid, then the top of the pyramid touches Thoth at 31° North, around his crown, while the Pyramid site looks out, over the delta, like the god. The geographical circumstances of the Egyptians appear astonishingly well arranged to suit their numerical beliefs and practices. Or were they "chosen" for just such a reason? Located on the longitude having the most land, placed in the center of Earth's land masses, living on a north–south river valley that provided waters in the desert while enabling easy triangulations down the meridian, it is small wonder that they would achieve great geodetic tasks while believing in their destiny to achieve them.

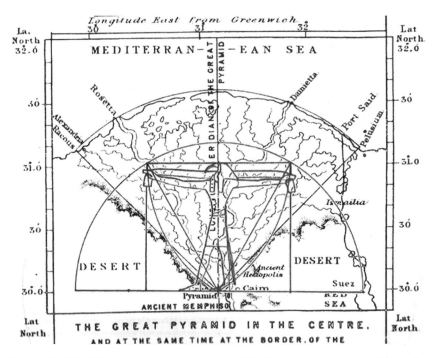

Figure 4.8. Thoth's iconography laid over the Nile Delta and the degree of latitude between 30° and 31°.

JERUSALEM AND THE NORTH

Just next door to the Great Pyramid is the more recent city of Jerusalem. It is not surprising that the metrology present in Egypt found its way into the layout of this archetypal sacred city, not least through the figure of Moses who, by all accounts, was trained in Egyptian priestly knowledge. The Jerusalem design is very ancient, and also has resonances with Stonehenge and megalithic Britain.

It is the Temple of Solomon that came to epitomize the secret sacred knowledge of the Jews. Destroyed by the Babylonians and again by the Romans after it was rebuilt, the site became a temple to Jupiter before transformation into the Dome of the Rock by Muslims. The Knights Templar (a Christian order of "warrior monks" that fought in the later Crusades) encamped there to create a medieval mystery, reputedly finding the sacred secrets of the temple. In recent times John Michell has identified the temple as present *in the layout of the city itself*,[2] a pattern six times bigger than the probable temple but having identical dimensions to its likely design.

The Bible is very unusual in that it often explicitly describes these dimensions as having been received from God. The pattern is of a rectangle twelve units by five units. The greater Jerusalem rectangle has, in each unit, 144 Egyptian sacred cubits of the *standard canonical sacred cubit,* 1.728 feet in length. The formula for this cubit is $2^3 \times 3^3/5^3$ while the temple itself would have had a unit one sixth of the city pattern, that is, twenty-four cubits per unit (fig. 4.9).

The symbolism of Jerusalem is complex, so just a few salient features will be highlighted here. As the rectangle is in a type of foot with no seven or eleven in its formula, the structure itself relates to the radius of the mean Earth. Three units from the west is Golgotha, where Adam's skull was traditionally placed, and three units from the east is the Rock of the Foundation. Between these is a length exactly 1/14000 of the mean radius of Earth ($1/(2^4 \times 5^3 \times 7)$). As with the base

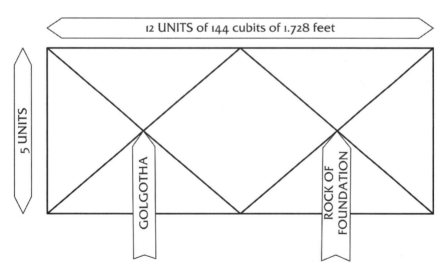

Figure 4.9. The plan of the city of Jerusalem, six times greater than the Temple of Solomon and anchored between Golgotha and the Rock of Foundation (after John Michell).

of the Pyramid, therefore, the side of twelve units represents the mean diameter of Earth.

But the rectangle is familiar both from megalithic Britain and as a container for the second "Pythagorean" right-angled triangle with side lengths 12:13:5.* We should note that each unit of the Jerusalem plan is 144 cubits and hence the twelve side is 12^3 cubits long or 1,728 cubits of 1.728 feet. This alone validates the metrology.

The same rectangle and hence triangle is found at Stonehenge between four stones called the "station stones." The distinctive Sarsen circle is enclosed by it, the twelve side being just ninety-six megalithic yards of 1.728 times 11/7 feet long. This "astronomical megalithic yard" or AMY, rediscovered as a unit by Robin Heath, is obviously a polar unit since it contains 11/7 within its formula. The AMY is 19008/7000 feet long, which is also the sacred cubit of 1.728 but multiplied by 11/7 to create a polar measure. The harmonic component is identical to the Egyptian sacred cubit as $2^3 \times 3^3/5^3 = 1.728$, but that is not the only strange similarity.

There are 7,680,000 AMY in the polar radius. Half of the twelve side at Stonehenge, which is forty-eight AMY, divides into the Pole 160,000 times, which compares to the 14,000 with which Jerusalem divides the mean Earth radius of $12^6 \times 7$ feet.

The AMY emerges from a direct relationship between the Moon and Sun, demonstrated best within this 12:13:5 "lunation triangle" pioneered by Robin Heath, for he has shown that the intermediate hypotenuse formed to the 3:2 point of the five side generates a length that accurately represents the number of lunar months in a solar year.[3] Making a lunar month one megalithic yard long, this length is 12.369 yards long; the 0.369 is the mismatch between the lunar and solar years, which happens to be *exactly one foot long* if the AMY is used (fig. 4.10). Thus the AMY relative to the foot is the ratio of the month to the difference between the two types of year, lunar and solar. This forms a direct link between cosmology and metrology.

---

*The square of twelve is 144; adding the square of five, that is, twenty-five, equals 169, which is the square of thirteen, a number with a bad reputation as unlucky.

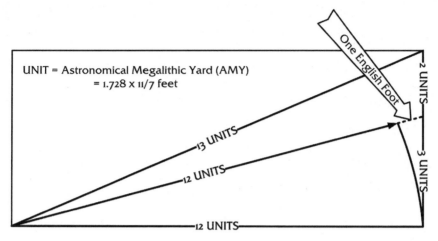

Figure 4.10. How the two 12:13:5 triangles fit the temple and the 3:2 point yields 12.369, the number of lunar months in a solar year, while the AMY generates the English foot when one AMY is equated with one lunar month.

In his latest book, *Powerpoints,* Robin Heath shows how the lunation triangle operates within the Temple of Solomon where the intermediate hypotenuse crosses the centerline at the "Holy of Holies" and terminates at the otherwise oddly placed Throne of Solomon (fig. 4.11). It was on this centerline that the sacred marriage of the Lord and the goddess Shekhina was the prime aim of yearly ritual. The implication is that the harmonization of Sun and Moon was seen as directly following the geometry of this triangle and rectangle, and that the ritual elements connected with objective time cycles naturally became couched in the design of the geometry itself.

The fact that two monuments so far from each other in their time of construction and location on the planet have a common geometric plan, in appropriate units, to two prime elements of the same ancient model of Earth suggests that a long-standing global tradition was at work, made up exactly along the lines reconstructed by John Michell and John Neal.

The connection between Jerusalem and Britain is mythically stated in stories like the northern visit of Joseph of Arimathea or even of Jesus, which could point to there having been a connection thousands of years

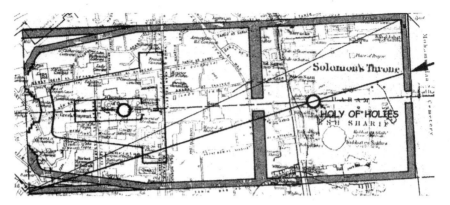

Figure 4.11. Kaufman's Temple Plan overlaying the city plan of Jerusalem, with the lunation triangle revealing the Holy of Holies at the centerline-intermediate hypotenuse junction, and Solomon's Throne at the 3:2 point (from Powerpoints *by Robin Heath, courtesy Bluestone Press).*

ago between the eastern Mediterranean and Hyperborea, the northern land near the Arctic that the Egyptians knew of, where Apollo was born and where the archaic astronomers, the Titans, were banished by the Olympians (fig. 4.12). In Hyperborea the world pillar stood on an island (compare to Atlantis, named after Atlas, the heaven bearer) suggestive of Britain and the Baltic as being the legendary Hyperborean land (adapted from Jurgen Spanuth[4]).

However, there is a simpler connection, in that *the degree of latitude at Stonehenge is the length that every degree would have upon the (perfectly spherical) mean Earth,* an Earth that is the prototype of the ideal within metrology, which is also true of Jerusalem, the Great Pyramid, and the City of Zion.

THE STONEHENGE-AVEBURY COMPLEX

There is a megalithic complex around Stonehenge that has, in recent years, revealed a large corpus of metrological information, including many examples of the ancient model itself. First, there is the monument itself, a set of rings and stones that interlock various radii, circumferences, and their interrelationship in a clear model of Earth and refer-

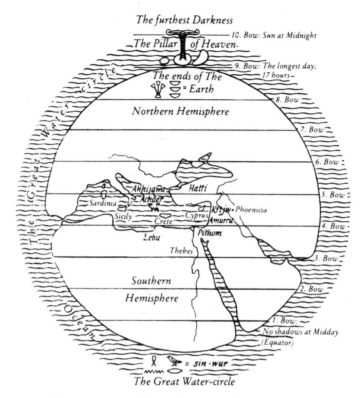

The furthest Darkness

10. Bow: Sun at Midnight

The Pillar of Heaven.

9. Bow: The longest day;
17 hours

The ends of The = Earth

8. Bow

Northern Hemisphere

7. Bow

6. Bow

5. Bow

Aḫḫijawa   Hatti

Sardinia   Achḥei

4. Bow

Sicily   Kftjw · Phoenicia

Cyprus

Crete   Amurru

Lebu   Pithom

Thebes

3. Bow

2. Bow

Southern

Hemisphere

1. Bow:
No shadows at Midday
(Equator)

= sin-wur

The Great Water-circle

Figure 4.12. The Egyptian worldview from around 1200 B.C.E. illustrates the "circle of the Earth" surrounded by the "great water circle" (Okeanos). In it the world was divided into nine bows (compare to latitudes of the Northern Hemisphere), at the top of which lies Hyperborea.

ence point of metrological standards.[5] At the same time the monument is aligned in multiple ways to the horizon and the calendar of the Sun and Moon.[6] These facts can only be selectively related here to suit our purpose of providing an integrative overview.

Directly north of Stonehenge is Avebury, the largest henge monument in Britain. It is located upon the Michael Line (a line connecting several sanctuaries dedicated to St. Michael, discovered by John Michell, see next chapter). Recently, Stonehenge and Avebury have been found to be connected by a geodetic triangular model of the polar, mean, and equatorial radius.[7] The equatorial hypotenuse of this triangle passes directly through Silbury Hill while Avebury itself marks the mean Earth

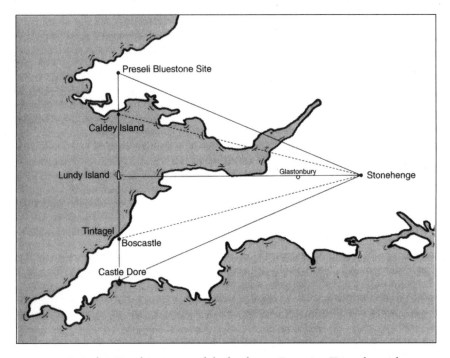

Figure 4.13. Robin Heath's picture of the landscape Lunation Triangles with Stonehenge at their vertex, connecting Lundy and the source of the bluestones of Stonehenge in a structure 2,500 times larger than the Station Stone Rectangle at Stonehenge. Lundy to Stonehenge is exactly 108 royal miles. See also figure 4.18.

radius. How this is achieved illustrates the ancient metrological process (fig. 4.14).

In English feet, the foundation stone of the metrological system, the polar radius, measures numerically 440 times 1,152 times 288/7 feet. These are the numbers available for work within monuments modeling the Pole, but in Britain the monuments have manifested as large triangles within the landscape, requiring less building and just the essential long-distance surveying techniques for Earth measure. The monuments themselves are predominantly flat circles of upright stones, post holes, or the banks and ditches that surround such stone circles to form henges. Long distances between monuments, as with long sightlines for sky angle alignments, allow high accuracies when modeling Earth.

In the Pyramid, a 440 to 441 relationship was used in its height; the

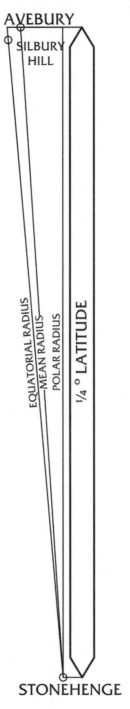

Figure 4.14. Layout of Stonehenge-Avebury Landscape Triangle.

441 could have been tilted from the base until level with the 440 "polar" height to yield a triangle. It could have been drawn upon the land to avoid building a large pyramid and this, it appears, was the thinking in megalithic Britain. It means that we are fortunate to discover these triangles since generally it is the monuments alone that get our attention. The Great Pyramid now appears less of an experimental work-in-progress and more a *tour-de-force* for the metrological culture.

The metrological key for the Pyramid is the Sumerian foot, one of which then gives the 440:441 relationship of pole to mean Earth. A 288:289 triangle with apex at Stonehenge gives a very accurate value for the equatorial radius in the 289 side if the 288 north–south base is the polar radius.[8] A number of measures can be used to yield interesting results but here we propose the Roman foot of 24/25 feet because then:

- The common unit of the triangle's sides is 330 Roman feet.
- The outer circumference of the Sarsen Circle at Stonehenge is 330 Roman feet.
- Silbury Hill is 288 Roman feet in radius.

The Roman foot is 5:6 of the canonical Egyptian sacred foot of 144/125 feet, the cubit of which is the now-familiar 1.728 feet. The monument at the apex, Stonehenge, gives the key as for the Sumerian foot in the pyramid, but here it is a longer composite length. The monument (Silbury Hill) on the 289 "equatorial" hypotenuse has a radius of 288, indicating the nature of the triangle being used, a 288:289 triangle.

Obviously, such a solution would require another, different triangle to relate the Pole to the mean Earth, since the main Avebury henge carries that relationship relative to the Stonehenge meridian traveling north. A 440:441 triangle is indicated by the ancient model, and this can be doubled to 880:882, allowing a further 883 hypotenuse to then model the equatorial radius. However the accuracy is then not so good, that is, the numerical properties of 883 are inadequate, since 883 is a large prime number unrelated to the early numbers used within the megalithic system. Also, the equatorial radius signified would then be too small. John Michell's final solution for this monument was to adopt a 264:265 triangle to map the ratio of polar to equatorial radius, but expanding this by five and allowing a 1320:1323:1325 triangle to be formed. This *fitted the monuments on the ground better* and gave an accurate model of the three key radii of Earth. Michell gives the key unit as forty royal cubits of 1.728 feet, which equals seventy-two Roman feet, one fourth of the radius of Silbury Hill.

How it works: 1,320 is three times 440 while 1,323 is three times 441, meaning that 1320:1323 is exactly 440:441. Dividing 1,325 by three yields 441 plus 2/3, which is larger than 441.5 (883/2) and gives the better estimate for the equatorial radius. The solution found by Michell and probably the megalithic designers was that 264:440, being a ratio of 3:5, gives a method of generating a third radius for the equatorial radius, using an alternative triangle of 264:265. The resulting length times 1600/7 gives an equatorial radius of 3,964.6753 miles.

DIMENSION	ANCIENT	MODERN	DIFFERENCE	ERROR
Equatorial Radius	3,964.6753	3,963.207	−1.468	99.923%

Some strange results emerge when looking at the quarter degree of latitude. The average degree is 69.12 miles long, which divided by four yields 17.28 miles (note similarity to 1.728 foot cubit) which is 52,800 cubits. Dividing by 440 gives units of 120 cubits each. Dividing by 264 gives units of 200 cubits each, so that each triangle allows division, using these cubits, of the quarter degree. The 440:441 relationship gives a polar to mean Earth radius model of 52800:52920. The 264:265 triangle gives a polar to equatorial radius model of 52800:53000. Both triangles are operating at the same scale of 1600/7.

THE METER: A LOST ANCIENT MEASURE

While the model of Earth is a clear demonstration of metrology, it is not the only ancient application of it. Since metrological units have only come down to us piecemeal, it is possible that there are units we have never identified. One such I discovered by applying metrological proce-dures to a megalithic complex that had been analyzed using the modern meter as a unit.

The meter has a peculiar legacy within France. Carnac in Brittany—perhaps the world's largest megalithic complex—has been studied for its meaning by a non-academic group there (*Association Archeologique Kergal* or AAK). Using the meter for their measurements, they discov-ered number symbolism indicating that it was the meter that had been employed by the builders. The meter, on analysis, appears to be a sys-tematically changed version of a demonstrably ancient measure that has been lost until now, partly because of the use of the meter.

The meter has a relation to the Persian foot of 21/20 feet, in that when multiplied by 25/24, the result is remarkably close to the meter, systematically different by a factor of 8,001 to 8,000. The former num-ber is sixty-three times 127, so that one can suggest that the French meter was perhaps "deliberately" related to an ancient measure of 105/32 (of which there is no record today), which I have labeled the "inverse Ibe-rian yard." The Iberian foot of 32/35 can be transformed with 21/20 into 24/25, the Roman foot, which, in turn, is transformed into the Eng-lish using 25/24, and into the Persian from the English using 21/20.

An "inverse Iberian" is then generated with a further 25/24, to cre-ate a completely symmetrical set of five measures with the English foot in the center. But, there is no record of it historically. However, there might have been *had the French meter not been invented*. After its intro-duction, any ancient site utilizing what appeared to be the meter in its metrology would appear to have been employing it before it was even established—an *anachronism!*

Who would have suspected that the new measure of the meter, designed to replace all the measures of the ancient world, had been based upon an actual ancient measure used in France during megalithic times? But it is not so surprising, considering that Napoleon's cohorts were deeply into secret societies and France was and has remained a major center for secret knowledge and groups such as the Knights Templar, the Benedictines, the Cistercians, and the builders of the Gothic cathedrals.

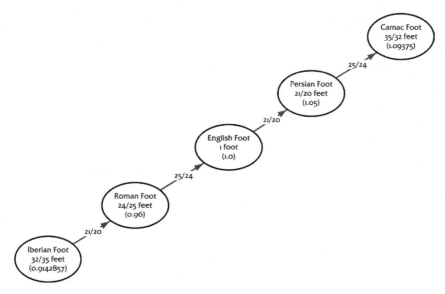

Figure 4.15. The progression from the Iberian foot to that found at Carnac (the inverse Iberian), through other ancient measures. The Carnac measure has been impersonated by the meter divided by three (that is, its foot) being only one part in 8000 different, and has the inverse formula of the Iberian.

Armed with this "new" ancient measure, almost identical to the meter, the megaliths of Carnac can perhaps be understood in a new way. While models of Earth are not yet accepted by modern archaeology, the metrology and purpose of the whole area around Carnac was explored around 1970 by the independent researcher, Alexander Thom, a leading engineer of his day.[9]

Thom had detected the megalithic yard in Britain following his accurate site surveys of megalithic stone circles, which revealed an apparent quantum of measurement.[10] He used statistics to prove that units close to 2.72 feet were widely used in Britain during the megalithic culture. The generation of this measure is most simply seen as a yard of Iberian feet, that is three times 32/35 of a foot.*

---

*Note that the Iberian foot leads to the megalithic yard while the astronomical megalithic yard, AMY, is of a similar length but related to the Drusian foot (root 27/25 feet) as a "pace" of 5/2 such feet (2.7 feet) multiplied by 176/175 and is then a polar measure with 11/7 in its formula. The Iberian, like the royal foot, has just 1/7 in its formula.

While the Carnac site is very complex, it is fundamentally tied to the measurement of the angular range of sunrises and sunsets during the year. At spring and autumn equinoxes, the Sun rises and sets directly east and west, while at winter and summer solstices the Sun has moved south or north, to form an angle relative to the east-west line of the equinoxes.

Relative to east and west, at this latitude, the solsticial location of the sun on the horizon forms a 3:4:5 triangle. This is special because it is the first triangle in the number field to have three whole number sides. The Bay of Quiberon appears to be perfectly adapted to form the sightlines required to study both the Sun and the lunar maxima, based upon 3:4:5 triangles, by employing a single sighting menhir at Lochmariaquer (fig. 4.16). For example, standing on the Quiberon peninsula there is a specific alignment from which this now-toppled Grand Menhir would have been silhouetted before the rising Sun in the winter, weather permitting.

The *Association Archeologique Kergal* had a measurement for the five unit side of the triangle, to Quiberon, as 16.8 kilometers. This makes the three unit side 10.08 kilometers. The formula within Neal's grid for a standard canonical variation within any module of measure is 126/125, which is 1.008 in decimal. If a measure is increased in this way by 1.008, then the measurement taken is reduced by the same proportion. Dividing 10.08 kilometers by 1.008 leaves the three side of the triangle as being ten kilo yards, if the meter is actually three feet of 35/32 (the inverse Iberian foot).

This means that, after applying the standard canonical variation, the three side is exactly thirty *kilo feet* in length. Thus this part of the monumental complex has been built to exactly ten kilo feet, equal to the Pythagorean units of the triangle in question. The chance of this occurring by chance is astronomically small. It confirms both:

- Thom's primary hypothesis about the site regarding its use for solsticial alignments via the unique 3:4:5 triangular alignments only at this latitude
- The existence of an ancient measure, 35/32 feet in length, that was evidently employed in Carnac

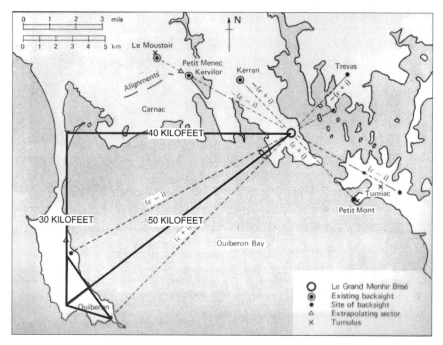

Figure 4.16. Quiberon Bay and Carnac megalithic complex embody the angle of a 3:4:5 triangle in the solstice-to-equinox solar alignments at just that latitude. The topography is strangely suited to the task.[11]

This inverse Iberian foot (yard = 3.28125 feet) can be confused/interchanged with the meter, which is one part in 8,000 different (meter = 3.28084 = 10000/3048 feet).*

This application of metrology at Carnac[†] illustrates how much remains to be found using these principles within the archaeology of ancient sites. Given accurate measurements and alignments, one can soon detect elements belonging to the numerical arts, but likely present in new and unusual ways. The costs associated with such analyses are far

---

*3048 lunar orbits accurately take twelve times nineteen years to complete and nineteen years is the period (known as the "Metonic") after which the Sun and Moon are in the same positions relative to the stars.

†Another example is the stone rectangle of Crucuno whose dimensions are three and four in units of ten megalithic yards, making the diagonal five units, reminiscent of the station stone rectangle that encapsulates the second rather than first Pythagorean triangle, twelve, thirteen, five.

less than scientific analysis of burials and general excavations, a point proved in that metrology has developed to this extent with no funding from any traditional body, generally no encouragement, and sometimes disdain. One wonders what it takes for the metrological paradigm to gain the notice of the scientific community.

AN AXIS OF THE MEGALITHIC

The Brittany region of France is a very strange special case. For instance in the fourth century C.E. Welsh monks and their entourage traveled by boat to repopulate Brittany, leading to the p-Celt population and customs (similar to Welsh traditions in dress and mythology) that are found there today. It was the backward nature of the area that partly protected the stones of Carnac. They were accessible only by rough tracks until the later nineteenth century.

However, the first group of megalithic people arrived there before the earliest phase of the building of Stonehenge. At that time they built strange tumuli of quartz rocks, such as the Tumulus of St. Michel, according to a four kilometer grid.[12] They also built burial chambers like those of New Grange, an example being found on the island of Gavrinis, four kilometers east of the Grand Menhir. The Gavrinis monument has a sophisticated arrangement in which the axis of the entrance tunnel is aligned to the Moon's maximum standstill, while the Sun at solstice sunrise was just visible along the long diagonal of the tunnel, seen from the main chamber (fig. 4.17). A threshold stone at Gavrinis is part of a similar stone at New Grange, while the roof stone is one part of an engraved stone used in two other locations within the complex.

Around 3400–3200 B.C.E., a catastrophe may have forced people to stop the developments around Carnac. The Gavrinis dolman was filled by fine sand and it appears the megalithic people withdrew from the area for centuries. When another megalithic phase began, it was to build the more familiar monuments of the Grand Menhir, and the stone rows or alignments, whose function revolves around the movements of the

Figure 4.17. Inside the spectacularly carved corridor of the Gavrinis Dolmen.

Sun and Moon. There is evidence that the stone rows tracked multiple calendars, including an unusual one of forty day periods that create a yearly calendar based upon nine such periods within 360 days.

Judging from the carvings on the walls of Gavrinis, the first phase of megalithic activity appears to have been geodetic, devoted to establishing some kind of a metrological grid, and concerned with the mysteries of Earth energies. The links between several megalithic complexes support this. Orkney, for instance, is on the same longitude as Carnac, as are Edinburgh and Cardiff. That is, these places are *on the same north–south meridian*. Rosslyn Chapel, the subject of much speculation, is also to be found on this meridian.

It is as if the Carnac to Orkney north–south line formed a datum for the megalithic world rather like the Greenwich meridian does for us today. For example, the meridian passing through Britain leads to a strange relationship between the lunation triangle—an artifact of megalithic society in Britain—and one of the catastrophe theories involving displacement of Earth's pole. As mentioned earlier, the lunation trian-gle exists within the diagonal division of the station stone rectangle at Stonehenge and equally, in the layout of the Temple of Solomon.

In deciphering this connection my brother Robin Heath first noticed that the transport of the bluestones to Stonehenge from their source in Wales defined a larger geodetic triangle with Lundy Island as its right angle. The distances involved in this triangle are 2,500 times larger than the station stone rectangle version.[13] In figure 4.18, point A shows Stonehenge itself and B the outcrop where the bluestones were sourced. Directly west of Stonehenge is Lundy Island, so that the lunation triangle relating to the bluestones has a Stonehenge to Lundy distance of 108 royal miles or 240,000 megalithic yards.

Robin then noticed that Edinburgh–London–Cardiff formed a fur-ther exact lunation triangle 2.5 times bigger than the "bluestone" one. I calculated the Edinburgh to Cardiff distance as being 270 royal miles. In addition, the famed "Royal Mile" in Edinburgh is a royal mile long, based on plausible points in the Castle and Abbey/Palace complex. The Royal Mile is in fact a natural "crag and tail" structure from a recent ice

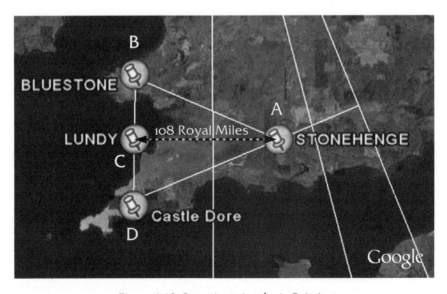

Figure 4.18. Lunation triangles in Britain.

age in which debris are deposited on the lee side of the crag by a glacier that passes it. It must have formed a natural processional way to Castle Rock from the north of Arthur's seat in megalithic times to what is now the castle site. Thus it should be seen as a powerful, natural landscape temple. The other large triangles encountered between Stonehenge and Avebury evidence the placing of reference measures as the length, radius, or perimeters of monuments.

The other interesting fact is that Edinburgh and Cardiff are on the same north–south meridian. Both lunation triangles were therefore oriented to east–west and north–south. In order to make a connection between them it is necessary to form the mirror image of the bluestone triangle, with a line running from Land's End in Cornwall, through Stonehenge to North London (somewhere around Hampstead Heath) (fig. 4.19). The line from Edinburgh to London becomes the twelve unit side of a new lunation triangle, with length 288 royal miles long.

This length of 288 royal miles is exactly 1/12 of the polar radius of Earth, within the ancient model. Furthermore, 288 divided by twelve yields the common unit length of this triangle's sides as being twenty-four royal miles. The triangle is in a 3:8 proportion with the bluestone

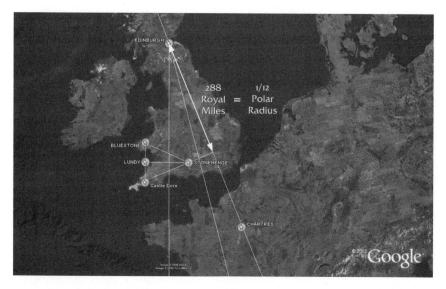

Figure 4.19. Aligning Stonehenge to the Edinburgh–Carnac meridian.

triangle while the new triangle is 270:288 relative to the Cardiff triangle, a proportion of 15:16, which is a half tone in musical harmony and the proportion of the lunar year to Saturn synod.*

Two interesting pointers emerge: The first is that the signature angle of around twenty-three degrees north of east is found as the average for the stone rows of Carnac. The second is that the line from London to Edinburgh, as a great circle, passes through the Yukon—the supposed location of a previous North Pole for Earth, approximately 100,000 years ago according to the contested theory of polar displacement. The placing of a polar length of 288 royal miles, 1/12 of the polar radius, pointing toward a previous polar direction might support the theory and help interpret the enigmatic presence of these large landscape triangles in Britain.

In the next chapter, the link between myth as the repository of pre-historic knowledge and geomantic lines upon the landscape is reviewed, because elements of these procedures have also come down to us in how sacred centers are established and connected to each other.

---

*A further 288 royal miles along this line reaches Borges cathedral in central France, which the Apollo Line also passes through. Peter Dawkins has traced the line from Scotland to the Gulf of Lyons in his *The Grail Kingdom of Europe.*

FIVE

MYTHIC HEROES AND GEOMANTIC TECHNOLOGIES

It takes a special effort to see that the world is rebuilt inside our brains. Though our brains are not directly in contact with the "out there" of Earth and cosmos they generate the necessary illusion so that we think we are. In this sense meaning is not a given but is always *made,* by influences such as expectations and worldview. In the past such meaning-making took many forms, such as geomancy and oracles, which in turn relied on an immense mythic framework that was itself a universe of meaning. Such myths were at least partly rooted in the numerical character of the universe.

A numerical view has the advantage of being able to be generated from direct observation using the human senses; it does not require technological instruments of measurement. While science has analyzed the world with such instruments, it has left us with a net feeling of insignificance in that we do not then have a *given* role within the universe. The death of the Creator God is the death of his creatures in the sense of their intended role within an earthly creation.

Some would argue that this loss of role is only the death of superstitious belief that led to wrong-doing, suffering, and needless destruction visited upon other humans. Yet the scientific view has proven no better, as it is directly involved in continuing warfare, competition, mismanagement, and erosion of Earth's primary systems of weather, biodiversity, and evolution itself.

The key advantage, then, of taking a numerical view of the world is that the human role is meaningful within it. It enables Earth to be connected to the sky, that is, to the cosmos. It also became associated with widely held ideas about the afterlife. Only a practical investigation of this worldview can reveal what the payoff was in terms of how it made the ancient peoples feel. The numerical view could have formed a natural portal to higher intelligence, knowledge, and consciousness. Once upon a time it could have been satisfying in itself and not *superstitious* at all.

Broadening the point, it is salutary to consider all worldviews as a form of *enchantment*. The nation states of today, the norms of education, the idea of globalization, even the concepts of product placement: these are all forms of enchantment too, and effectively in the hands of a priest class. From this perspective, enchantment suggests the hypnotic influencing of others, rather than the effect of an uplifting environment.

The enchantment of the ancient world was a worldview articulated in an encyclopedic oral tradition, an edifice that has survived even down to the last few centuries because of the appeal of such stories. Traces of them can be found in many places, but the Indian subcontinent has the purest rendition of the oldest periods of Indo-European development because a priest class, the Brahmins, effected the transfer of scrupulously reproduced oral material into writing.

In the West the story of King Arthur, which extended over a thousand years, incorporated many elements of these stories. While the outer story seems to drink from the font of Christianization, at its heart lie far older frameworks such as the Celtic. A closer look will reveal the cosmological and numerical basis of many aspects of the myth.

ARTHUR: A PRECESSIONAL AND POLAR MYTH

Everyone has heard about King Arthur and his twelve knights. As an enduring myth, this story gives us episodes that in fact belong to separate

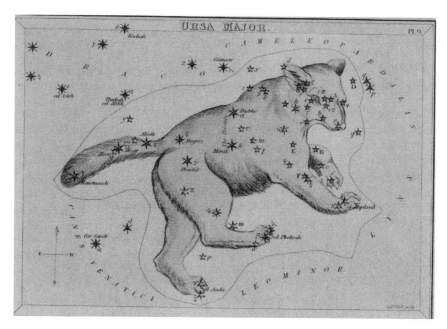

Figure 5.1. The constellation of the Great Bear whose seven primary stars form a tail and lower back. Until recent times it was also called Arthur's Wain, as it circles the celestial north pole.

ages: prehistoric, post-Roman, early medieval, late medieval, and "modern" versions of the "Matter of Britain" as the corpus has come to be called.

To discover the *prehistoric* aspects of the story requires some study of etymology and also of the powerful archetypes that preexist within myth itself, as it relates to the starry sky.[1]

Arthur is connected to bears, the Welsh *Arth* meaning "strong like a bear." He is also commonly associated with a star constellation, once known as Arthur's Wain ("Arthur's Way"), and now called the Great Bear (*Ursa Major* in Latin) or the Big Dipper in the vernacular (see fig. 5.1).

Yet another name for this constellation is The Plough, for the reason that these seven strongly visible stars rotate* (in our age) about the celestial north pole (of our age). The Hindus called it the Seven Rishis,

---

*In Welsh "turn" is *troi,* leading to symbols such as a Plough of the Sky and the "troy pattern" labyrinths.

which connects with a very ancient idea that the "mountain of heaven" had seven layers, leading naturally to the concept of a stepped pyramid, such as the ziggurats of ancient Mesopotamia. From the model of Earth described in chapter 3 it is clear that the symbolic meaning of seven with regard to the Pole runs very deep.

The Great Bear is being hunted by the herdsman Bootes, who follows on behind. The chief star of this constellation is called Arcturus, from which the name Arthur is also sometimes thought to derive. A clearer derivation might be the Arctic, which in the sky is the region of circumpolar stars. These stars are "immortal": they never set, although they become invisible by day. They rotate endlessly in the north for dwellers in northern latitudes. Indeed, in the Arctic region, the majority of stars are circumpolar and the mountain of heaven becomes a literal truth.

In this mythic world of phonetic resonance and similar motifs, variants of the same story exist in many regions. Myths bypass official history because their framework belongs to our prehistoric subconscious of primordial categories, even though they are seemingly inconsequential and often dubbed as "children's stories."

A basic understanding of the concept of *precession* will help make the mythical references clearer. In general, precession refers to a change in the direction of the axis of a rotating object. The axis of Earth undergoes such a change due to a combination of Earth's non-spherical shape and the gravitational forces of the Sun and Moon applying torque as they attempt to pull Earth's equatorial bulge into the plane of the ecliptic.

As a result of precession, the celestial north pole moves in its own cycle of (traditionally) 25,920 years ($2^6 \times 3^4 \times 5$). It is therefore a location—rather than a pole star—around which all the stars rotate once a sidereal (measured by the stars rather than the Sun) day (fig. 5.2). A few polar stars, like the present Polaris, punctuate this circular progress of the pole in the sky. The center of this polar motion is an invisible point called "the pole of the ecliptic"; it is the pole of the solar system itself seen from Earth, which lies at a ninety degree angle to the path of the Sun, or ecliptic.

As it happens, the pole of the ecliptic is actually marked by the

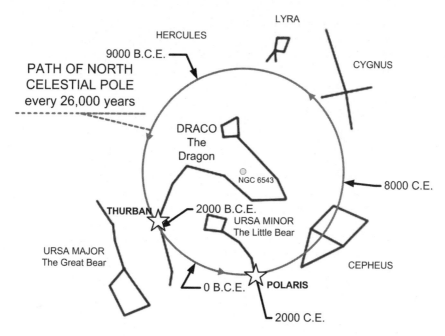

Figure 5.2. The path of the celestial north pole due to precession.

unusual Cat's Eye nebula NGC 6543 (fig. 5.3). This NGC number is easy to remember since it is the size of the polar radius of 3,456 royal miles in reverse.

The Cat's Eye nebula is surrounded by the constellation Draco, the Dragon. The ecliptic pole literally pierces the dragon's body, an illustration of our contention that the Arthur myth—in which the dragon is a central motif—has deep roots, in heaven as on Earth.

The position of polar star often lies vacant for thousands of years, leaving just an invisible point to *hold up* the sky. On the celestial *equator* —Earth's equator projected into infinite space—we today place twelve regions within the Sun's yearly motion through the stars, called the zodiac.

Earth's pole is tilted, however, so the zodiac circle and that of the celestial equator are split apart and touch only at two points called "nodes." These nodes are our spring and autumn equinoxes. The tilt of Earth's axis leads to the excursions of the Sun above and below the celestial equator and thus to the heat of summer and cold of winter.

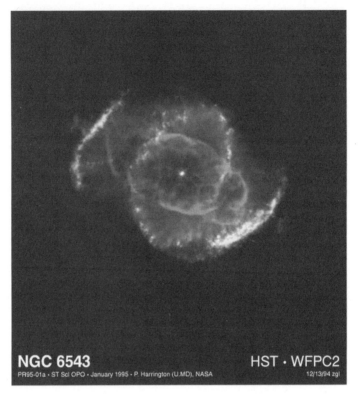

NGC 6543

PR95-01a · ST ScI OPO · January 1995 · P. Harrington (U.MD), NASA

HST · WFPC2

12/13/94 zgl

Figure 5.3. The Cat's Eye nebula that lies close by the ecliptic pole.

The precession of the pole over 26,000 years means that there is also a *precession of these equinoctal points* within the zodiac. The whole precession is called the "Great Year" since the movement of the equinoctal points relative to the Sun strongly resembles the motion of the Sun, day by day, within the ordinary year.

The movement of the nodes through the zodiac divides the precession up into "precessional ages" of 26000/12 years long or about 2,160 years. These ages are identified by the part of the zodiac where the vernal equinox falls. With this in mind we can say that Moses lived in the age of Aries the Ram, Jesus was born into the Age of Pisces, and that we are currently approaching the Age of Aquarius.

The precession of ages within the Great Year created the concept that life on Earth was different in different ages, a mythological concept of history couched in terms of eternity, that is, of pure recurrent patterns. While history is typically driven by the day to day, linear concept of progress, eternity says "there is nothing new under the Sun." From this eternal perspective of great time, in which one degree shift in the Sun's equinoctal point equals an entire human lifetime of seventy-two years, what happens on Earth is viewed as a tragic inevitability in which mythic heroes have to die, the righteous be usurped from their rightful places, and a search for redemption begun as the land lies wasted. These are all themes developed in the myth of Arthur.

There is good evidence that the precessional myth became humanities' largest and most enduring myth. It can be identified in many cultures, in the Pacific, the Andes, China, and Africa, as well as Northern Europe. As a greater form of astrology, various temple precincts could have measured and tracked it. It took the seminal book, *Hamlet's Mill,* to identify this mythic prototype, which pushes back the horizon of meaning for humanity deep into our prehistory.

However, academia has had the same problem with *Hamlet's Mill* as it has with metrology and the model of Earth: if some of our oldest symbols are derived from precession, then who measured precession in prehistory?*

In fact the story of Atlantis itself is partly a precessional myth because its end involved one of the catastrophes generated by the great wheel of precessional time. The king who ruled Atlantis was Poseidon, who was to become the god of the sea for the Greeks. While he then became the brother of Zeus, he was actually a precursor figure—like the Saturnian Kronos/Chronos—always built into later myths and who passes on the framework of power before withdrawing. As Peter Stewart puts it: "There are many stories of 'first emperors' who retire from their worlds to rest 'in the depths'; King Arthur is only one of them."[2]

The falling of gods, kings, and dreams is tied in precessional myth

---

*Hipparchus was the first historical figure to be credited with noticing precessional movement, through the systematic errors caused by it in older star measurements. Interestingly, he came from a satellite town to Tarsus where the precessional cult of Mithras was developed and where the prototype of Mithras, Perseus, was worshipped. These two represent the same constellation, called Perseus today.

to the submerging of certain stars below the celestial equator. In these myths, the stars are like a realm of potential action and meaning for an age. The starry sphere was split into above and below, into heaven and hell, Olympus and Tartarus: realms that endure in the theological ideas of the monotheist dualists.

Whereas equatorial stars fall down or rise up (the original meaning of the word *disaster*, "falling star"), the celestial pole perpetually falls because it eternally circles the Ecliptic Pole as a planetary orbit circles the Sun. The pole is therefore tragic in that its round is fated, generating the fate of risings and fallings on Earth. To go beyond fate, therefore, is to go beyond this creation; such a concept has at its heart a form of Gnostic belief that the creation is flawed and imprisoning to the human spirit.

The ancient ideas of resurrection were naturally tied to the great circles of the celestial equator and ecliptic and to the seasons. The Sun—the archetypal hero and ruler—dies in autumn when it dips below the celestial equator, and is reborn in the spring, progressively as one travels further north. In this way the pole and the equinoctal and solsticial points belong to the same phenomenon and give the Sun a *different kind of light* from that of the nurturing heat normally associated with our own star.

If the dead are to travel "back out" of this creation they must do so along the great circles of celestial equator, ecliptic, and thence to the great galaxy; this was the theory symmetrical to any belief in astrology, since birth was inferred as the reverse. In Indian tradition (related in the *Shatapatha Brahmana*) the dark half of the year was called *pitriloka*, the place of the fathers or ancestors, while the light half was the *devaloka,* or place of the gods. The barrow within which the megalithic buried their dead usually pointed to the winter solstice. The process of leaving and returning to Earth was the subject of dream narratives such as the Dream of Scipio, or of Socrates looking at Earth from space; it is also possible that the seven and eleven level labyrinth designs were a manifestation of the planetary levels or beyond, making the journey in and out explicit symbolically.

The Sun, archetypal hero and ruler—set in the context of his age by precessional reality—is subject to awkward reversals of fortune that then destroy one vision and require that a *quest for new meaning* be initiated. In this sense, the historic growth of the Arthur myth from the story of a Celtic-British warlord to a courtly Christian king with twelve knights came to include the trappings of precessional myth. These prehistoric elements *found a haven* within which they were both appropriate and authentic. This implies that *myth-making taps into archetypes* that can never be directly known but instead are to be inferred through knowable patterns that embody them.

This is perhaps an explanation as to why myths arise: They belong to a self-repairing species that derive their energy from experience, when informed in a way that can turn *imagination* into a vision of the archetypal pattern. Perhaps zeitgeists are archetypal creations.

ORACLE CENTERS AND DIVISION BY TWELVE

The archetype of the Pole is both a rod of measure related to the size of Earth's polar radius, and a literal pole in the ground representing the Pole as the giver of an inherited framework of creation. Such a pole forms a *center* that is a representative of the Pole and as such can be given a zodiac. Poles were evolved as gnomon, shadow sticks, givers of knowledge through the interpretation of their shadow in the Sun, with the shortest shadow of the day pointing north to the Pole. Centers were also used as sighting markers for alignments to more distant markers.

We have already seen that the network of ancient sacred sites were connected to Earth, in position and size. What such centers meant has somewhat leaked into the present through the Norse practices of establishing centers, which continued within the historical period. We are fortunate that this source of ancient procedure has been collated and re-investigated by John Michell in his study of Centrism.[3] Centrism is a geomantic procedure whose last known use was in Iceland in 875, but the evidence then points to similar procedures in the Celtic and other Indo-European landscapes.

There is also strong evidence for centrism within the megalithic, one example being that Stonehenge is located halfway along the Michael Line but at right angles to it. Avebury is on the Michael Line but one quarter of a degree north of Stonehenge. The result is a root three relationship relative to the line's center, since the line travels at 60° east of north. The principles of finding a center seem to hinge on one or more lines that define the longest available length on land for a given region or island (fig. 5.4). Ideally this longest line is exactly north–south, but in some cases, such as shown on Islay, it may be the longest line possible in any direction.

It has been observed that the Isle of Man lies at the center of the British Isles. Seen in concert with the center line of Ireland, these irregular islands take on some simple geometrical meaning if one thinks of the Isle

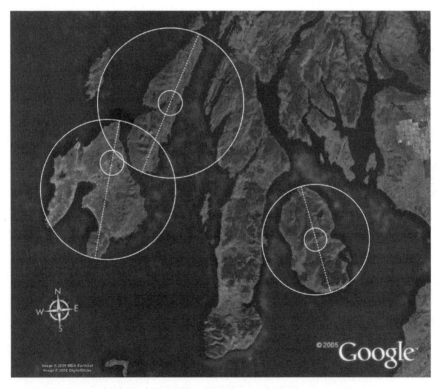

Figure 5.4. The southern Scottish islands of Islay, Jura, and Arran (left to right) with the Centrist geometry applied. On Islay, John Michell shows the location (circled) of Council Island on Loch Finlaggan, on this longest "center" line. The other centerlines are speculative.

of Man as lying at the center as an "organizing principle" rather than just by accidental geological circumstance (fig. 5.5).

Within the Norse tradition—which was carried to Iceland and many northwestern British islands—the aim was to establish, usually at the center of such a line, a Thing place (a place where the governing assembly of a "northern" culture met, made up of the free men of the community and presided by law-speakers, effectively a parliament or law-speaking place).

The surmise that these techniques are based upon what were megalithic practices is supported by the survival of these procedures of enchantment in recent times, in combination with the use of a twelve-fold

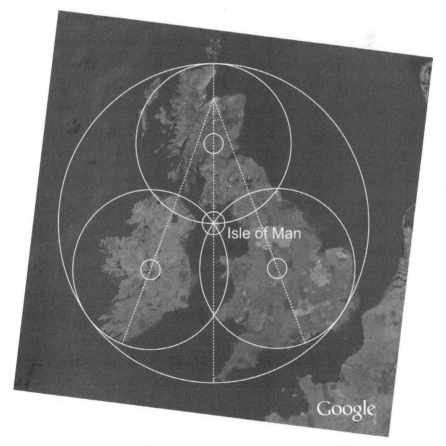

Figure 5.5. The centers of mainland Britain and Ireland reveal a surprising symmetry about the Isle of Man.

division of space about such centers, the association of Baltic peoples with both the megalithic and proto-classical Greek cultures, and the commonality of sagas and epic myths in their pantheons and motifs. Also of interest is the fact that observing from a center converts the skyline east and west into a calendar, between maximum Sun positions that correspond to the solstices of summer and winter (remembering figure 1.3). Megalithic tombs are generally oriented toward a solstice, to catch the Sun's light at sunrise or sunset. Thus, the basics of meaning for a center become associations of local land features with the sky, to which can be added geometrical and metrological relationships.

The advent of our zodiac appears to lie at the beginning of the classical period. Partly this is a tautology because historical records are obviously required for us to know of it. Less well known is that the familiar zodiac of twelve constellations was used to divide up local space into twelve directions, with lines traveling at thirty degree intervals from an oracle center, relative to the local horizon rather than the Sun's path. In the Mediterranean there is evidence that the oracular centers were in existence before the invasion of Indo-Europeans. However, it seems highly likely that the twelve-fold geometrical integration was imposed by the new arrivals.*

We are fortunate that the twelve-fold division of both peoples and places has survived in historic and monumental ways. The geometrical and numerical symbolism of twelve has been thoroughly studied by John Michell and Christine Rhone in *Twelve Tribe Nations*. The Athenians were divided into twelve. There is strong evidence of twelve tribes within the Celtic world. In Scandinavia, Odin had twelve followers or disciples (while hanging on the world tree to save the world, which sounds like Jesus on the cross). Iceland, Ireland, Isle of Man, and many places had

---

*It is significant that the children of Israel were organized as twelve tribes and that the Egyptians, while centered in their beloved Nile, had also been involved in the whole network of centers in this region that contained omphalos stones at oracular centers. These stones were geodetically organized according to the system of latitude and longitude that existed in prehistory, according to *The Sirius Mystery* by Robert K. Temple (Rochester, Vt.: Destiny Books, 1998).

twelve regions. King Arthur's round table had twelve or twenty-four places and twelve "knights, saints, hermits, and missionaries is a recurrent image in old British legends. Like the Grail it is associated with periods of regeneration and sacred order" as John Michell puts it.

Most of the above correlations are recovered elements from history and myth, which complement the origins of twelve-foldness found within number and astronomy. The works of Plato are a rare example of historical writings that are directly about numerical meaning. They contain an allegory that holds some numerical lore behind the twelve-fold division of a proposed human society called Magnesia.[4] Included are procedures for the finding of a suitable center, followed by the division of the directions by twelve gods. There is a ruling council of 360, evidently calibrating the circle itself into the familiar and perfect number behind the year, itself in perfect harmony with twelve (30 times 12), unlike the practical year of five times seventy-three days, that is, 365.

Plato's account complements the recovery from another Indo-European source, the Vedas, of similar knowledge of harmony and number,[5] from a different branch of their diasporas from the north. All that could be known about harmony was contained in these works, including knowledge of the even-tempered scale only used in the West within the last 500 years. While twelve-fold organizations have been found in Africa, for example in Egypt and west Africa, in Madagascar, and Asia and Polynesia, the main transmission into history occurred through the Greeks. These disparate origins of twelve-foldness might imply a global phenomenon that had some common roots, at least in the numerical model of Earth, and possibly in a global culture such as the Atlantis also described by Plato.

The work of Jean Richer in particular has uncovered what must have been a monumental complex of temples, oracles, and astrological symbolism within the eastern Mediterranean. His work is complex but a major pattern, revealed to Richer in a dream, is the alignment of Delphi, Athens, and Delos along a "rhumb line," a line of a constant bearing of 60° west of north (fig. 5.6).

Richer described his process as follows:

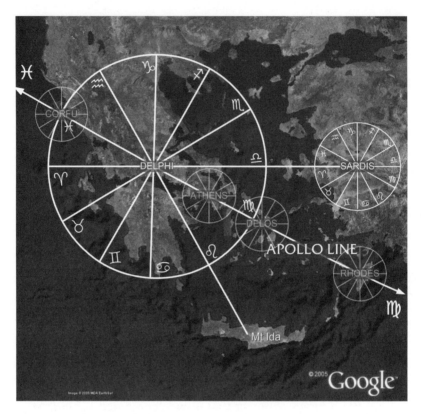

Figure 5.6. The twelve-fold pattern of centers near Delphi and the Apollo Line traveling east to Mount Carmel and west to Southern Britain. (After Jean Richer, Sacred Geography of the Ancient Greeks *[New York: SUNY, 1994].)*

For about a year I did no more than observe these significant alignments. In my first notes, nevertheless, I had already written:

"The Mount Ida–Delphi direction symbolizes the vital spirit of the country of Greece. This line intersects parallels of latitude at a 60-degree angle and may be considered as the projection over part of Earth's surface, taken as flat, of the Leo-Aquarius cosmic axis, which defines the same angle in relation to the line of the equinoxes."

This axis is the cosmic signature of Greece and makes it a mirror of the celestial harmony of the zodiac and the planets of the solar system (p. 4).

Periodical trips back to France, especially to Brittany, opened my eyes to a deep analogy between what I was observing in Greece and the almost unknown civilization that erected the megaliths.

The great solsticial alignments of Stonehenge, Carnac, Lagadjar, and the solar ritual of death and resurrection suggested by the drawings in the amazing tumulus of Gavrinis could help to reveal what may have been one of the secrets of Delphi. These solar temples were aligned according to a law.

From then on everything seemed to fall into place and it quickly became clear that the Greeks, like the ancient Mesopotamians and the Egyptians, had wanted to make their country a living image of the heavens.

A whole system of symbolic correspondences began to emerge, a system still somewhat fragmentary but already rather impressive. It suggested many relationships that were confirmed by certain divine or geographical names, by many coins and vases, and by poorly understood details of Greek religious history.[6]

THE APOLLO/MICHAEL LINE

Apollo, the Sun god, was born on the island of Delos and so the particular line passing through Delphi, Athens, and Delos has been called the Apollo Line,[7] as shown on the figure. It potentially forms a twelve-fold pattern at other centers through which it travels. This gives the opportunity, objective or subjective, and possibly both, for every center established on radiating lines to re-emit the original pattern of twelve directions.

The choice of Apollo for naming the line comes from his association with these places. At 36° latitude, between Crete and mainland Greece, the Sun rises in winter exactly along the Apollo Line, at 30° north of east. Therefore, when viewed from Athens and Delphi, the Sun god is literally rising in Delos, his birthplace, at the winter solstice. In fact it is on the island of Rhodes, a little further southeast, that 30° exactness occurs; thus the Sun god is born (starts the new year) at Mt. Carmel on December 21, though his official birthday was December 25.

The oddness of the Apollo Line is the fact that in Richer's zodiac of Delphi it represents two astrological signs, those of the Fishes and the Virgin. This alignment represents the exact equinoctial signs of the precessional age of Christianity: Pisces (at the vernal equinox) and Virgo (at the autumnal equinox). The iconography of the Church evolved in perfect resonance with these signs, in respect to the virgin birth and the initial letters of "Jesus Christ, Son of God, and Savior," which spell Ichthys (ΙΧΘΥΣ) or "fish," the symbol used by early Christians as a secret sign. This and many other factors created implicit linkages between the symbol and sign of the precessional Age of Pisces and the religion of Jesus that would dominate the culture of Europe in the following millennia (fig. 5.7).

As the Apollo Line (defined by Delos, Athens, and Delphi) extends into Italy it strikes Mount Gargano, the site of an important shrine to St. Michael, Monte Sant Angelo (fig. 5.8). The peaks, wells, and caves along the line have also been associated from time immemorial with Gargan, the giant gargantuan that symbolizes Earth energy; they are also thought to have been significant to the goddess beliefs of the ancients where Mother Earth was expressed within the landscape, the crust of Earth. In a non-dualistic sense, both light and dark, male and female, would be seen within the landscape.

The Apollo Line *became* a Michael Line in early medieval times at Mount Gargano, which formed a major staging post for any pilgrimage to Jerusalem. It was here in the early tenth century that Norman knights (formerly Danish Vikings) paid a visit. This led to two vital steps in western Europe's history:

- The Norman knights met the Benedictine order of monks who managed the shrine to Michael and they invited them to re-establish Mont St. Michel on the western edge of Normandy, itself on the Apollo Line. Mont St. Michel became a destination in the world of medieval pilgrimage.
- These knights were invited to help liberate parts of southern Italy, whereupon they discovered a power vacuum within which their

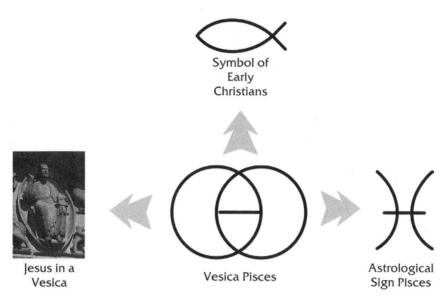

Figure 5.7. Jesus the Pisces or Fish, the symbol of Vesica Pisces transformed into the star sign Pisces, was an early secret sign of Christians and was heavily employed in the medieval Church as a symbol of Jesus, Lord of the World.

Figure 5.8. The Apollo Line in the eastern Mediterranean basin enters at Mount Carmel and then goes through Rhodes, Delos, Athens, Delphi, and Corfu. It enters Italy at Mount Gargan where a primary grotto to St. Michael had been established by the Benedictine Order after the customary "killing of a giant" and "falling of an arrow" motifs.

fighting skills and unique system of affiliated warriors enabled them to conquer all the southern parts including Sicily. This in turn enhanced papal power in Rome, a power that would subsequently launch the Crusades. In the course of their conquests, they came to occupy most of the lands at 36°, including Aleppo, Cyprus, Malta, Corfu, Rhodes, and Libya.

The Benedictine establishment of centers follows geodetic principles belonging to a previous age, though the accompanying mythology took the form of stories of arrows landing, or of bulls being slain or simply resting at the spot where a center was to be founded. As Paul Broadhurst says, "There is an unwritten tradition that the Benedictines preserved the knowledge of earth energies from former times."[8] What would otherwise have been a rejected *pagan story* was therefore reused, as were the locations in question, which became the powerhouses of the new belief system. This story is taken up in the following chapter.

Pressing on in this brief overview, from Mount Gargano, the Apollo (now Michael) Line crosses Italy and then France, and continues on to pass through St. Michael's Mount in Cornwall, England, having crossed the Channel from the similarly named Mont St. Michel (fig. 5.9).

As the Apollo/Michael Line crosses Britain, it also crosses (at St. Michael's Mount) what is known as the Michael Line of England, which passes through some of the most important megalithic and ecclesiastical monuments and foundations in Britain such as Glastonbury, Avebury, and Bury St. Edmunds. This Michael Line travels 60° east of north rather than 60° west of north. It falls short of marking the summer solstice and instead aligns with the path of the Sun's light at the May quarter day in the old calendar (fig. 5.10).

As soon as the Dukes of Normandy had reestablished Mont St. Michel, Duke William pressed his rival claim to the English throne, enforcing it with ships and armed knights. Through good fortune, they arrived days after King Harold's armies had fought a heavy battle against the Danes to the north. The day was lost to the Normans after a pivotal instance of the feigned retreat (a famous ploy of steppe horsemen). The

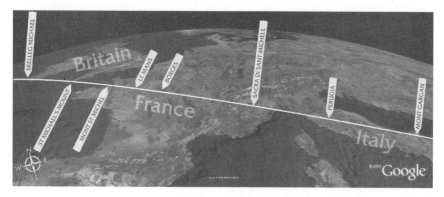

Figure 5.9. The Apollo Line enters France through northern Italy, passing through Borges, Le Mans, and Mont St. Michel. Traversing the English Channel to St. Michael's Mount it continues to Skellig Michael, a rocky Atlantic Island off Ireland's southwest coast.

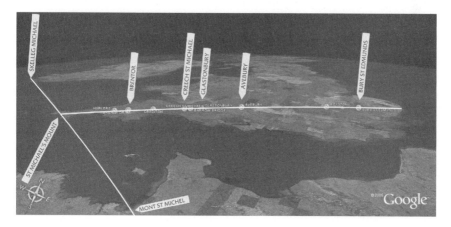

Figure 5.10. The Michael Line traversing the longest available straight path within southern Britain.

Benedictines came to Britain, which led to the rededication of Apollo-like sites such as St. Michael's Mount in Cornwall.

THE ARCHANGEL, "SAINT" MICHAEL

Both Apollo and Mercury/Hermes, with whom he is often equated, were members of the classical Greek pantheon of twelve gods. Although their equation is traditional, it hides differences between them that reflect

Figure 5.11. St. Michael from The Apocalypse of St. John *by Albrecht Durer. (Courtesy of Connecticut College.)*

the changes in society at the time and that followed a largely Athenian model. The Sun god Apollo was associated more with the priesthood and aristocracy, who were under attack from a new middle class of crafts- and tradesmen, associated with the subsidiary deity Hermes/Mercury, who was the Sun god's "right hand man."

In the Christian pantheon—in which one God had become three-in-one plus angels and saints in various formats—the archangel Michael took over the mantle of the subsidiary Sun god. This complicated theogony is remarkably compatible with the classical and pagan worldview and came about through Greek and Roman influence upon the early Christian system of beliefs. In fact the idea of angels hails from the Persian tradition and their subsequent inclusion in later messianic phases of the Jewish experience B.C.E.*

---

*The religion of the Persians was another variety of Indo-European thought, which would re-emerge in medieval times as the Cathar heresy.

The Persian religious figure of Mithras could be said to prefigure both Michael and Jesus. The name Mithras has an ancient provenance, being seen also as Mitra in the Vedas. While the iconography of Mithras is of killing a bull rather than the dragon slain by St. Michael, this is because Mithraism was a precessional cult[9] (fig. 5.11). The precession "kills" the previous precessional sign and its cultural norms; the sign of Taurus that was current when the megaliths were being built was "killed" by Mithras as the constellation now called Perseus (fig. 5.12).

Perseus (Mithras) is also the Greek hero who kills Medusa and holds

Figure 5.12. A Tauroctony (killing of the bull) of Mithras is essentially the constellations Perseus and Taurus, according to David Ulansey. The cross-legged attendants have upward and downward torches representing the ascending spring equinox and descending autumn equinox, respectively. (Fresco of Mithra, Dura-Europos.)

her head in his hand *while looking away*. Other variants of this motif include Indra who slays Vritra, the cosmic snake, causing the Sun to be held up high—a reference to the tilting of the Pole and separation of the ecliptic and celestial equator. The serpent-woman Medusa, the snake or python, the bull, and the dragon all represent the matriarchal, Stone Age past and the old world of Earth mysteries. Snakes were traditionally looped around geodetic stones, along with nets and grids. They were also associated with the "temple prostitutes" who were displaced by Athena, the transformed goddess; she established a cult of virgins who carried snake baskets into which they could not look. The symbolic ascendance of the Sun god is a natural expression of the rise of a patriarchal society. Thus the Indo-European invasion is suitably represented by *Apollo Killing the Python* at Delphi (fig. 5.13).

The widespread cult of Mithras was especially popular within the Roman legions, which is why three temples to Mithras have been found on Hadrian's Wall, and why Jesus was given the December 25th birthday

Figure 5.13. Apollo seated on the Omphalos of Delphi and stretching his elbow to kill the Python with an arrow.

Figure 5.14. Mont St. Michel, France's greatest tourist stop, with a figure demonstrating distinct characteristics of Mercury, including a hexagonal shield and ceremonial flame sword.

of Mithras. Thus it is not surprising that Mithras became the archangel Michael, born from a rock and in the service of the light. In chapter 7 Michael is further linked to the inner planet Mercury, who is a "guardian of the pathways" in traditional lore. His command of the medieval pilgrimage network is signified by his iconography placed everywhere upon churches, and not just those upon identified Michael Lines (fig. 5.14).

The association of Earth's energy with dragons makes the St. George version of Michael especially appropriate. St. George—who was brought back from the Holy Land by crusading knights to become the patron saint of England—carries a Norman lance, which represents the straightness of the solar rays that penetrate the dragon, the dark energies of Earth.

Michael took on a dual role, as both warrior of the Church and he who *weighs the soul after death on scales,* a picture more familiar from Egyptian iconography of Maat, who also measures the soul (fig. 5.15). This symbolism is related to the ancient concept of the Stoics that humans came into creation and re-ascended into heaven via the pathways of the sky. However, the origins of the iconography became detached from its usage, the meaning entering the collective unconscious.

The congruence of Apollo, Michael, Mithras, and Perseus are clear even though they differently kill a snake, a dragon, a bull, and the Gorgon respectively. The targets together are parts of a single whole: a prehistoric culture under attack from a patriarchal society from the North. These same themes are manifested in the myth of King Arthur.

Figure 5.15. Portal Relief Saint Michael Chapel, Kassa, Hungary 1360–70.

ARTHUR THE CELTIC BRITISH WARLORD

The story of Arthur forms a link between the dark age of post-Roman Britain, where it began, and the medieval age that would come to define the emergence of the great and the good along the lines of armed horsemen, as the essential aristocrats to rule over nations (fig. 5.16).

After the eventual demise of the Roman Empire there was a great power vacuum in Romanized Britain. The Romans left a swathe of people stranded at a level of material organization unmatched by their neighbors. Compare this with the Celtic peoples of Britain who largely derived from the megalithic peoples, who had been annihilated, marginalized, or integrated by the Roman assault upon their druidic religion. The newly emerging Christianity was at this time portrayed in the form of the Celtic Arthur, who can be placed in Scotland as a historic reality.

This early story is of the reintegration of a people by a warlord, fighting a set of land-grabbing barbarians and establishing a new kingdom of stability. The role played by mounted cavalry in the story of the strategic victory is odd. Although we are used to warriors on horseback, from the medieval period to "cowboys and Indians," such horsemen were not indigenous to post-Roman Britain. The armies of classical times were

Figure 5.16. One of the oldest depictions of a knight from the Sassanide relief. The figure on top in the middle is believed to be Khosrow II. The figure to the right is Ahura Mazda, and to the left is the Persian Goddess Anahita. The identity of the knight is not known, although various theories exist, but he is certainly of royal nobility. (Courtesy of Wikimedia Commons.)

made up of foot soldiers and chariots rather than cavalry. However, there is some good evidence that the Romans had brought them from their eastern frontier to guard Hadrian's wall. How that came about has been reconstructed by Howard Reid in his book *Arthur, the Dragon King*.

Mounted cavalry had arisen on the steppe grasslands that cut a vast swathe, southwest to northeast, through Europe. Riding should be compared to sailing as a key historical technology. For horsemen the steppes were "motorway" and "service station" combined, leading to rich but pastoral communities to raid or rule over. There have been many such bands of horsemen. For example, the Greeks feared the Scythians who were wise but a threat; they were portrayed as the half horse, half man centaurs. Russia was established by Scandinavians who invaded the Black Sea via the Dneiper, the Cossacks being their elite force of cavalry.

Nomadic fighting groups were used by the Romans as a unique weapon to defend their borders. The Romans had come up against the Sarmatians in Croatia, where a Roman victory led to the Sarmatians providing a force of 5,500 heavy cavalry auxiliaries to protect Hadrian's Wall. There is no evidence for their return from Britain and we know that auxiliaries were generally retired locally and given title to land. This makes the Sarmatian descendants good candidates for any well-trained horsemen appearing under the leadership of a King Arthur figure. The traditions of the Sarmatians and other steppes horsemen such as the Alans, has given rise to the proposition that their traditions were the successor to a classical model for governance adapted to a patchwork of minor rulers. Since these Caucasian steppe people had strong links with Scandinavia and the Indo-European diaspora, then the combined skills of horse and boat found, for instance, in the Norman conquest of Britain in 1066, yields some additional meaning (see next chapter). The Sarmatians wore fish-scale amour, making the confusion of the medieval knight with the older stories in the Arthur corpus natural and appropriate (fig. 5.17).

Figure 5.17. Sarmatian horseman with fish-scale armor and a lance.

Figure 5.18. King Arthur in combat, brandishing a draco windsock pennant that, like Draco, is proximate to a pole, in a natural precessional motif. (From L'Histoire de Merlin *by Robert de Boron, 14th century.)*

Other symbols provide congruence between steppe horsemen and the Arthurian traditions:

Courtly behavior: Women are treated differently in a nomadic culture.

Feudalism: The feudal system of collecting rents and tithes from conquered agricultural peoples was an evolved form of pillage.

The dragon motif: This has been equated with the characteristic red pennants of the Sarmatians that made a whistling sound when they charged in battle (fig. 5.18).

Grail traditions: Drinking the blood of livestock from a cup is common in nomadic nations, as was using skulls as cups.

The story of Arthur can be seen as having revolutionary resonances in that the structure of the future is present within the earliest versions of the story, making it almost ahistorical, out of time and place. The story then was retold in a way that made the Saxons, the Angles, and the Jutes enemies of Arthur, in fact enemies of the Plantagenet Norman kings of England. This allowed the story to absorb stories from local non-Christian roots. Unlike the Danes from Denmark these Danes and Norsemen from France (the Normans) had quite possibly absorbed the horsemanship of the Alans in Brittany, the same Alans who had helped devastate Rome and dominate, with the Visigoths, Spain and North Africa.

The Normans influenced the medieval reworking of Arthur's tale, which had come to Brittany (William the Conqueror was one quarter Breton) through its occupation by the Welsh (see pp. 177–81). Arthur's story belonged to the *p-Celtic language group* whose people now occupy Wales, Cornwall, and Brittany. When p-Celts were forced out of southern Scotland post-Arthur, the story naturally traveled to Wales. Some of these Welsh, then also under pressure, colonized Brittany in the fourth century, so that when Lancelot turns up in Brittany or Arthur at Mont St. Michel (to kill a giant ogre) there is no discontinuity in mythic terms—Scotland, Wales, Cornwall, and Brittany were all p-Celt lands around the time of the original Arthur. By medieval times, the Angevin Empire had carried the scope all the way to the troubadour courtliness of Eleanor's Aquitaine, steeped in heretic freedoms of chivalry, and to the Pyrenees in southern France, just next door to the Gnostic lands of Cathar Languedoc.

Thus it is wrong to suggest that medieval versions of the Arthur mythic cycle were simple fancy or exploitation of themes by later cultures. The storytellers of the medieval age were directly connected to both the p-Celtic tradition and other soon-to-be destroyed mythic currents that included those of the steppe peoples, of southern France, and others who shared congruent traditions. Actually, the area of difficulty must have been to integrate the Arthur myth in what were outwardly Christian and Roman politics. However, the superiority of knights in the service of Christ, and nominally under the control of the Church, made it hard to declare Arthur's story heretical despite its Celtic or other inclusions.

SIX

SECRET MEN FROM THE NORTH

One of the mysteries of the Mediterranean occurs around 1500 B.C.E. It surrounds the decline of the Minoan culture, the reign of Akhenaton (the monotheist pharaoh), and the Exodus of the Jews from Egypt. The concept of monotheism, which would come to dominate so much of European history, arose about this time. The Minoans in Crete, the Egyptians in the Nile Delta, and possibly the Jews in Egypt were all affected by the massive volcanic eruption of Thera, also called Santorini (fig. 6.1). The eruption occurred between a radiocarbon date of 1600 B.C.E. and an archaeological one of 1450 B.C.E. It is sometimes also equated to the catastrophe that destroyed Atlantis since Thera was largely destroyed by this last major eruption.

Plato (427–347 B.C.E.) is the sole source of information on Atlantis: that it was a legendary island of high culture destroyed by fire and water, probably volcanic activity and deluge. As a legend it has naturally come to symbolize any such event in which a civilization is destroyed followed by a dark age. But when events in the Mediterranean are considered alongside other facts about the Atlantic coast and the megalithic culture spread along that ocean's shores, they reveal influences beyond the Mediterranean that were key to the changes that happened there.

Figure 6.1. The location and remains of Santorini, now called Thera. Santorini was completely central to the region between Greece and Crete. Its recently excavated capital Akrotiri was a great Minoan cultural center.

After the purely Minoan period (3000 to 1450 B.C.E.), and within five hundred years, Plato's culture had come into existence, with a completely new religious mythology, centered in Greece proper and thought to be underway by the time of Homer, in the seventh century B.C.E., and Hesiod, 700 B.C.E.

This classical system of thought introduced a twelve-fold set of Olympian gods that were led by Zeus, later titled Jupiter by the Romans. He had been "born" on Crete, which is where the Minoan culture had been centered. He deposed his despotic father, Kronos, who can be equated with Saturn, the God of Time.*

The Disk of Chronos (analyzed in chapter 1) that I found in Crete indicates that the time system of Saturn was in use there after the Santorini event. It is therefore most interesting to know how the myth that "Zeus deposed Chronos/Saturn" might have come to exist. Could it be an *oblique description of real events* occurring at the end of the Minoan period, as is often the case with myths in general?

THE END OF THE NEOLITHIC

The Minoans represent the modality of Neolithic culture called matriarchy, in which the leadership, secular and spiritual, appears to have come

---

*Macrobius equates Kronos with Chronos to complete the cycle of meaning that Kronos is Saturn (Chronos), the archaic god of time.

Figure 6.2. Ladies in Blue, Minoan fresco that adorned the large antechamber of the throne room in the east wing of the Knossos complex.

through the female rather than the male. There is widespread evidence for this culture, which had predominated in the lands surrounding the Mediterranean and Anatolia in Southern Turkey.*

The central plain of Crete is dominated by Mount Juktas, visible from the south portal of Knossos, the greatest of many Minoan "palaces" that were probably religious precincts of the matriarchs. Mountain sanctuaries such as Juktas are found throughout Crete, as well as Paleolithic caves used as shrines to the Mother Goddess from earliest times (fig. 6.2).

Knossos was mistakenly dubbed a "palace" by its discoverer, Sir Arthur Evans. He also derived the name of the Minoans from King Minos who figures in the classical Greek myth of Crete in which a half man, half bull eats young Athenians and lives at the center of a labyrinth. He didn't realize that King Minos was invented as a patriarchal distraction from the matriarchal truth. But the matriarchal Minoan culture

---

*Anatolia is thought to be the origin of the Minoans, possibly Catal Huyuk itself, based on obsidian finds.

was transformed soon after the Santorini eruption and an extraordinary period of earthquakes that preceded and followed it.

The Mycenaeans appeared as the Minoans declined (fig. 6.3). They were followed by other groups that invaded from the north—Dorians, Ionians, and so on, of whom some later became the Phoenicians and a major part of the classical Greek culture. Their culture was characterized by men, force of arms, and competence at sea, but where did they come from and why?

During a warming period after the last Ice Age, known as the "climatic optimum" (see box on page 118), many of Earth's great ancient

Figure 6.3. Death mask of Agamemnon, famous patriarchal king of the Mycenaeans, whose power expanded to fill the gap left by the downfall of the Minoans.

civilizations began and flourished. In Africa, the Nile River had three times its present volume, indicating a much larger tropical region. In the north the warmer weather of 4000–5000 B.C.E. meant that civilizations could prosper near and even within the Arctic Circle, and the Arctic Sea was navigable. These northern people have come to be called the Indo-Europeans, based upon their location in India and Europe during the historical period.

When the climate again became cooler, making the northern regions less habitable, they migrated south, leading to the *polar myth* of "men from the north." The earlier cooling period (3000 to 2000 B.C.E.) corresponds to the migration of a single group of people from the north into India and Persia (Iran). The later period corresponds to the arrival of the Dorians, Ionians, and others into the east Mediterranean basin. What must have been a large and varied culture in the far north is now known more through its descendant branches than through direct information about the culture itself.

With regard to the Indian and Greek Indo-Europeans two key markers attesting to their migration have been noted. In *The Orion* (1893) and *Arctic Home of the Vedas* (1903) B. G. Tilak notes that many of the symbolic references in the Vedas—written down between 1500–500 B.C.E. from an earlier oral poetic tradition—correspond perfectly to the celestial arrangements that would have been seen by an observer living near or within the Arctic Circle, in the age in which the constellation of the Bull (Taurus) marked the vernal equinox. This would place authorship of the verses in the north, between 4000–3000 B.C.E. Unfamiliarity with the sky phenomena of the polar region led to Tilak's theory being devalued as an unlikely fantasy.

Similarly, in *The Baltic Origins of Homer's Epic Tales,* Felice Vinci notes that the *geography* found within Homer's epics, *The Iliad* and *The Odyssey,* has always confused scholars, leading to its dismissal as being just inaccurate or created with poetic license. However, Vinci found the geography of these works fits very well farther north, leading to his contention that they refer to events that had taken place in the Baltic Sea *before* an Indo-European migration into Greece.

THE CLIMATIC OPTIMUM

By 5000 to 3000 B.C.E. average global temperatures reached their maximum level and were about seven degrees (Fahrenheit) warmer than they are today. Climatologists call this period the Climatic Optimum.

From 3000 to 2000 B.C.E. a cooling trend occurred. This cooling caused large drops in sea level and the emergence of many islands (Bahamas) and coastal areas that are still above sea level today.

A short warming trend took place from 2000 to 1500 B.C.E., followed once again by colder conditions.

Colder temperatures from 1500–750 B.C.E. caused renewed ice growth in continental glaciers and alpine glaciers, and a sea level drop of between six to ten feet below present day levels.*

---

*Abstracted from www.physicalgeography.net/fundamentals/7x.html.

The Baltic Sea is similar to the Mediterranean, being an inland sea rather than an ocean, and could have formed the western portion of an Indo-European homeland, whether along the Arctic coast of Eurasia or further south, near the Caspian Sea. The peoples of the Baltic migrated to the Black Sea and entered the Mediterranean via the Bosporus, shortly after the Thera/Santorini event. Other routes also existed for these migrations, through northern Italy and around the coast of the Iberian Peninsula (that is, via Spain). They were established *trading routes*, well known for the exchange of amber, bronze (copper and tin), gold, and products made from them. These *Amber routes* from the eastern Baltic naturally became available for migration.

Meanwhile, the strong seismic activity of that period was devastating the Minoans and other Mediterranean peoples caught between the African and European tectonic plates. As Santorini cast a lethal pall over eastern Crete and northern Egypt, two bastions of the old world, tsunami waves destroyed many Cretan ships and coastal settlements, and the Indo-Europeans moved south to colonize large areas of Greece and Turkey.

According to Vinci, Homer's epic tales are really ancient Baltic

Figure 6.4. Part of a miniature fresco of Akrotiri showing Minoan boats, from before the Santorini explosion.

sagas of people we would identify as Vikings, Danes, Jutes, Lapps, and Finns! After the southern migration, the places within these epics were adjusted to loosely fit similar topographies encountered in the Mediterranean. This might seem far-fetched but it is completely congruous with many other known factors of Scandinavian culture and climate. Vinci points out that the ships of Homer's epics have a design like that of the Vikings, including a distinctive removable mast. Although the Minoans were a trading empire based upon sea navigation around the coasts,* they seemed loath to represent their boats, despite their otherwise highly visual culture. Few depictions have been found as in the picture of Akrotiri, where the boats look more like gondolas than effective fighting vessels (fig. 6.4).

It appears therefore that the Minoan trading ships might not have had the business model of "trade with the strong and pillage the weak" associated with the later Vikings. And, as the Minoans didn't stray into

---

*Objects of Minoan manufacture suggest there was a network of trade with mainland Greece (notably Mycenae), Cyprus, Syria, Anatolia, Egypt, Spain, and Mesopotamia.

Figure 6.5. Battles with the sea peoples in the time of Ramasses III. (Funerary Temple of Ramasses III at Medinet Habu, battle approximately 1190 B.C.E.)

the Atlantic, their nautical skills and equipment would have been less developed. Thus, a superior vessel arrived in the Mediterranean from the Baltic. We know that by the period of Ramasses the Great (ca. 1279–1213 B.C.E.) there were problems on the coast of Egypt from "sea people" of a fierce disposition, wearing helmets with horns* (see fig. 6.5). These northern sea people merged with the Canaanites to become the loathed Philistines aka Phoenicians.

Sea power became the decisive power within the Mediterranean through the ages that followed: the Baltic peoples arrived with it; the Phoenicians replaced the Minoans to found Carthage and similar trading powers; the Cilician pirates near Tarsus in Turkey were a problem for the Roman Empire; and the Knights Templar developed a fleet to serve their logistical needs, centered on Marseilles. Sea power is connected with navigation, which means mapping Earth's surface and being able to travel reliably (and mapping in turn is inevitably associated with one's model of Earth). Portuguese portolan maps (navigation charts, dating

---

*The Vikings never wore horned helmets but the earlier Bronze Age peoples of Europe and Scandinavia did.

from the fourteenth century or later, in manuscript, usually with rhumb lines, shorelines, and place names) exist from a mysterious past culture. They showed the New World before it was "discovered," implying that old knowledge—which was plainly more relevant to the Atlantic coast of Europe than the Mediterranean—was mixing with new knowledge.

The Indian and Persian branches of the Indo-Europeans appear to have "sailed by land," using the steppes as an effective inland sea of grass. Mounted horsemen in armor, using the stirrup, appeared at the borders of the Persian Empire: the Sarmatian warriors that might have entered the Arthur story via the Romans. This steppe technology played a pervasive role in later history. The Sarmatians could be mistaken for later medieval knights as could the Alans and Visigoths who helped bring down the Roman Empire and dominated the western Mediterranean for centuries. Integrating with the aristocracy through gaining land or defining an aristocracy through conquest are much the same thing. In this way the static populations of the Neolithic became fodder for what evolved into a *feudal* culture with deeper roots than just the medieval.

A MERGING OF CULTURES

As the Indo-Europeans moved south, they brought with them a set of myths that are congruent across all of the groups that dispersed into Eurasia from the north. As their myths were already well defined, their migration created a discontinuity with the prevailing myths of already indigenous peoples such as the Minoans, Libyans, and Egyptians.

The Dravidians of the Indian subcontinent might be detected behind Yoga and the Agastya figure of southern India, but the Persians' precursors can only be guessed at because these migrations occurred millennia before that from the Baltic Sea.

The Egyptians were affected less than the Minoans by Santorini and the Baltic invasions. Their economy was based upon the fertility of the Nile and on gold to the south, beyond its Nubian headwaters. Their culture slowly declined, its vast legacy relatively unchanged but gradually losing its regional power.

In contrast, very rarely is a change of mythology so marked as it was between Crete (matriarchal Minoan) and Greece (patriarchal, from the north). Perhaps the Baltic Indo-Europeans had exceeded the Neolithic *through technological innovation,* particularly regarding the use of metals; it is very possible that such technology was the "tipping point" for the previously stable Neolithic societies based around women. The meeting and mixing of these two different cultures in the eastern Mediterranean basin made it a womb for the culture that evolved first into the classical Greco-Roman, then into the medieval Christian and subsequent scientific and technological cultures.

The new Greeks from the north quite obviously brought with them the twelve-fold zodiac and their twelve Olympian gods who replaced the Titans. A twelve-fold system of geodetic meaning was also extended around a number of established oracle centers.[1] The "new" northern mythology was "born," like Athena from Zeus' head, *fully formed,** which is why the Norse and Greek myths are so similar.

Matriarchy was often associated with the Saturnian year of 364 days plus one, the "year and a day," which brought an end to the reign of the Zeus-king, an official male who was sacrificed after just this duration. There is evidence that over time the power of the king whittled away at these rules, resulting in the substitution of a "great year" of 100 lunations (three times thirty-three plus one). The king may have even started to sacrifice surrogate boys in his stead, a practice that would naturally lead to a mythic Chronos who "swallows his own children." By some fluke a child sacrifice was preserved, in progress, by an earthquake at the northernmost part of the Mount Juktas† sanctuary peak. The story

---

*Zeus was said to have slept with Metis, the goddess of "crafty thought," but feared the consequences, perhaps because she represented the older goddess culture. He swallowed her, as his father was to have swallowed him, but afterward he had a big headache, relieved only when Athena emerged from his head "ready formed, armed and with a shout." This implies that Metis had been transformed into the ideal female within the new pantheon: a virgin goddess, rather like an Amazon, who was the patron of both war and learning.

†Yuktas and other variations of the Greek can be expected on English maps and books, the rule being phonetic equivalence.

of Zeus is thereby given substance as referring to the practice of sacrifice in the culture preceding that of Zeus.

The whole story of Zeus is enacted between palace, cave, and sanctuary once the mother goddess Gaia helps Rhea, his mother, to save him from his father's appetite for eating his own successors. A stone is offered, which Chronos duly swallows instead of the child, while Zeus, like Moses but in a golden crib, is hidden within the Dictean cave still found to the east, on the Lasithi Plain. The cave is typical of a limestone region, with stalactites and stalagmites that are evocative of forms emerging from the Creatrix of Earth herself (fig. 6.6).

Brought up out of harm's way, Zeus was able to depose the cruel king Chronos and the Titans from which he hailed, as foretold, and to establish the twelve Olympian gods from among his swallowed brothers, along with new fantastically transformed aspects of what had come before such as Athena.

Figure 6.6. The Dictean Cave, birthplace of Zeus on the highland Lasithi Plateau, Crete, and a sanctuary since the Stone Age.

In classical Greece a popular notion was that all Cretans were liars because they said that Zeus died in Crete. Although this was in harmony with the matriarchal tradition of the king sacrifice, it was anathema for the new pantheon of *immortal* sky gods of the Greeks and then Romans. Even St. Paul, a Roman citizen, repeats the charge. However, the recumbent body of Zeus can be viewed from the west of Mount Juktas as its ridge in silhouette, a familiar conceit concerning mountains in prehistory (fig. 6.7).

Between the fertile crescent of Mesopotamia and the Eurasian Steppes (Central Asia), a mighty Neolithic revolution had appeared that had clearly influenced the Semitic peoples too, giving birth to the twelve tribes of Israel. This was a true melting pot or even, as J. G. Bennett remarked, the cauldron that somehow fused various cultural influences into a modern composite culture, rather like the metal bronze that was revolutionizing the uses of metal, particularly through accurate casting of weapons.

The Indo-Europeans in the Mediterranean went on to be associated with an Iron Age that made still more devastating weapons, but the idea that they emerged in the Bronze Age—first as Mycenaeans and then other groups from the north—is thought provoking. It may also explain the rich Hellenic culture that emerged from a dark age to form the foundations of "Western culture." Greek culture looked backward to Atlantis through Plato and gave birth to the later mysteries of the medieval such as sacred geometries in the Gothic cathedral.

Figure 6.7. The recumbent form of Zeus found in Mount Juktas in Crete where the Cretans claimed Zeus had died. (Photo courtesy of Joanna Charlton.)

ATLANTIS ON THE ATLANTIC

The idea that Atlantis was a culture that somehow centered on the Atlantic coast of Europe is a well-developed one—even the name helps. It leads naturally to the idea that the megalithic culture found on the Atlantic coast must have been a manifestation of whatever Atlantis was. Either the megalithic came about after the destruction of Atlantis, or was left behind after that culture had passed away. It is clear that the last minor constructions at the Stonehenge site were around the time of the Thera/Santorini explosion, about 1500 B.C.E. Before that, megalithic structures were built over a period of prehistory lasting many millennia, with many massive henge structures having been built over a thousand years before the initiation of the outer ditch and bank of Stonehenge.

What then is the connection between Atlantis and the Baltic culture? The megaliths stretch at least from Portugal in the south to Sweden on the Baltic. If Homer's epic is relocated according to Vinci's hypothesis, then traders and adventurers of the Baltic world also navigated the British Isles and even the Faeroes. They obtained tin from Cornwall and the Scilly Isles, and were trading via the Thames. Therefore it is not conceivable that the megalithic peoples were different from these seafarers. The megalithic culture was both Indo-European and whatever Atlantean means, too. Also, the mention of the use of tin and the existence of metal weapons, smiths, and so on within the stories of Homer implies that the Bronze Age was under way for these peoples many years before they had to migrate to the Mediterranean.*

This is all an embarrassing re-write of history. It means that the short stretch of water from Bronze Age Crete to Greece and its Iron Age Aegean culture is a larger cultural discontinuity than was thought. It means that the classical culture was largely a graft of the northern culture of peoples forced south by a worsening climate.

---

*The name of the most famous smithy was Lemnos, an island in the Aegean Sea. However, in the work of Vinci this translates to an island off the coast of Finland and Sweden called Lemland.

It appears then that some Baltic (= megalithic = Atlantean = Indo-European) peoples went overland using the Dneiper, to enter the Black Sea, with a portfolio that already included bronze weaponry and a great facility with ships.

The name Indo-European derives from the idea that the Indians, named after the Indus river, were found to share language roots with Europeans. Perhaps this culture should really be called Atlantic-European. On the other hand the megalithic could have had a precursor or partner in culture close to the Arctic Circle; thus the Atlantic Ocean, along with the Baltic and Arctic Seas could at one time have been their domain.

A SEARCH FOR THE MIRACULOUS

John G. Bennett—in his life's work to interpret the spiritual history of the last ten thousand years—encountered Tilak's books on Aryan roots. Bennett's basic intuition was of four major cultural centers having been set up after the descent of a new kind of power into the human, that of the demiurge or maker. The demiurge is an angel who brings the world into existence, along with its evolving living cargos and, through this work, the human experiment with consciousness. His idea was that each of the four different groups were given a different aspect of the whole to focus on; as a result, they produced different ideas about god or the creation in the late Stone Age.

While the major focus in Bennett's work was on *implicit* cosmological ideas that hail from the numerical cosmologies, these sit well alongside the numerical arts seen in monuments. Since cosmologies present the world as the product of Higher Intelligence, God, and so on, and since this work of creation could be a continuous one, this is an idea relevant to human evolution itself.

To the author's surprise, Bennett wrote articles on both Santorini[2] and the hyperborean origin of the Indo-European peoples.[3] While he thought that geophysics and human history might well be entwined, he felt Atlantis was on Crete rather than elsewhere and did not connect the late Indo-European invasion with Santorini, as we have here. It appears that only recently have enough parts to this puzzle become available to make my own conclusions possible. Bennett also explored the evidence from the three main language groups, including the Indo-European, observing that it takes a mighty circumstance to create a new language. This is an achievement no one in the modern age has been able to come close to and we can certainly see it as another indicator of past creative skill.

One of the principles of intelligence is that origins that are simple on a cosmic level become complex and dense when seen on an existential level, that is, when manifest on Earth as complex systems. The return to simplicity, as an original formative pattern, could possibly be behind the creation of twelve-fold structures of meaning, laid out in landscapes by the Atlantic-Europeans. One reason why such simple structures might have been used to organize their world is that higher energies have to do with *consciousness* rather than materiality. Bennett found some evidence for number acting within systems of meaning and developed his Systematics of systems up to the number twelve, which the reader will find an extraordinarily familiar idea from the previous chapters.

The debunking of ancient spiritual modalities by moderns very likely comes from an inability to discover such higher organizing patterns within experience. Science discourages the search for patterns, calling it a *selection* process in which one finds what one is looking for, having rejected other equally valid data. However, this argument assumes that all data is content neutral and not a carrier for higher energies or levels of order. It is subjectivity, a property of consciousness, and not objectivity that appears to be active in the dream life and in waking intuitions of patterns within the complexity of the world.

History is actually full of "miraculous transformations" and "enigmatic movements" that, after the fact, are wrongly seen to be the only way things could have happened. The point of "alternative history" is to intuit the "motivation of history" as if one had to organize or design it, which a hidden influence could in effect be doing, human or superhuman. Such a thought experiment gives us a role in working with historical information that is usually reserved solely for historians. This may account perhaps for the recent popularity of alternative history as a genre.

In the history we are reconstructing here, the Atlantic peoples came into contact with the goddess culture and subsequently dominated an "old world" of the eastern Mediterranean and Egypt. Akhenaton's obsession with the Sun and Moses' flight out of Egypt (into monotheism of a more abstract kind) may have been connected, since monotheistic religions appear to develop both political and ecclesiastical patriarchies.

The Apollo (Sun god) Line introduced in chapter 5 may seem an unlikely construction yet it does represent, at Delphi, one of the thirty degree lines of the twelve-fold division of space that again relates to the invading northerners. At one end of the Mediterranean, Mount Carmel was a sacred site in prehistory that historically came to represent the Holy Land, being called the "Holy Head" by Tuthmoses III. As mentioned earlier, it lies on a line passing through Delphi, Athens, and Delos. This Apollo Line then meets the thirty degree line in southern England known as the Michael Line (see chapter 5). The extrapolation of geodetic ideas points to the possibility that this line, that travels through Italy and France to reach southern England, indicates something historical.

As we have seen, the Apollo Line passes through a very significant island on the coast by Normandy, called Mont St. Michel, before it reaches England. It is here that the Duke of Normandy invited the Benedictine Order to re-establish the abbey, after the Normans had encountered the Benedictines on the eastern coast of Italy, where they ran a major Michael shrine.

It is significant that the name *Norman* means "man from the north." Its derivation is linked to the Vikings' movement from the north (Denmark) when they first attacked France. Denmark is very significantly the entry to the Baltic Sea, guarded by the strait of Elsinore, where the castle of Shakespeare's Hamlet was located. Also, the British Michael Line, after leaving eastern England, passes through Denmark, into southern Sweden, across the Baltic to Lithuania.

When the Normans attacked Paris, their very real threat was contained through a deal in which they consolidated their lands in what is now Normandy in exchange for integration with the French state as vassals of the king. They officially became French and Christian, though for two generations they still spoke Danish.

When Norman groups in Italy aided the pope and conquered much of southern Italy and Sicily, they gained influence with the Church and freed it from immediate threat. The losers were the Lombards of northern Italy, the Eastern Church of Constantinople, and a Muslim caliphate. Soon after this consolidation, the First Crusade was declared that would galvanize northwestern Europe.

Through the post-classical Dark Ages, the Benedictines and their predecessors had acted to preserve knowledge in monasteries that were fortified retreats. They collected and reproduced documents during a period when these would otherwise have been destroyed. As the Benedictines emerged into the Middle Ages they appear to have had secret knowledge about the network of pagan sites, some of which lie on the lines of twelvefold and other patterns that emanated from and linked important sacred sites throughout the ancient world. Their knowledge guided the selection of sites that were reasserted as sacred during the medieval age, by having

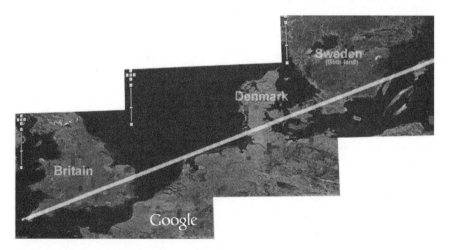

Figure 6.8. Continuing the British Michael Line into the Baltic and the "arctic home of the Indo-Europeans."

churches and cathedrals built upon them. The traditional explanation is that the Church merely wanted to overlay "pagan" sites to obliterate their influence and redirect these visible landmarks, but in so doing they were also continuing the pagan traditions themselves, even though they evoked angels and saints instead of their direct antecedents.

With the blessing of their patrons, the Normans, the Benedictines were established on a key point on the Apollo Line at Mont St. Michel, where they created what must be one of the most remarkable sights in the world—a spiritual fortress (fig. 6.9).

William the Conqueror even met with King Harold there, before the 1066 invasion of England. William was a valid heir to the English throne and this invasion resulted in the consolidation of all the lands between the Apollo and Michael Lines, Normandy and southern England. Perhaps this means nothing except, for instance:

Two of the greatest early Christian establishments in England lie on the Michael Line: Glastonbury and Bury St. Edmunds. As soon as William was established, he had problems in the north with one of the strongest earls, Northumberland. This led to devastation from York-shire up to Durham, and to the establishment of a unique combined

Figure 6.9. Mont St. Michel in 1900. Some early Gothic elements were created in the lower chambers of this fortified holy island dedicated to Michael.

princedom and bishopric at Durham. A grand cathedral was also built there and Benedictines installed. A line at right angles to the Michael Line, departing from Bury St. Edmunds, locates Durham, which is also directly north of Mont St. Michel (fig. 6.10).

Durham Cathedral has the first Gothic ribbed vaulting that actually strengthens a vaulted ceiling enough to make it capable of supporting a stone roof. This was an important improvement since the wooden roofs of earlier cathedrals were regularly destroyed by fires. The experimental origin of this key Gothic ribbed vaulting technique can be seen in Mont

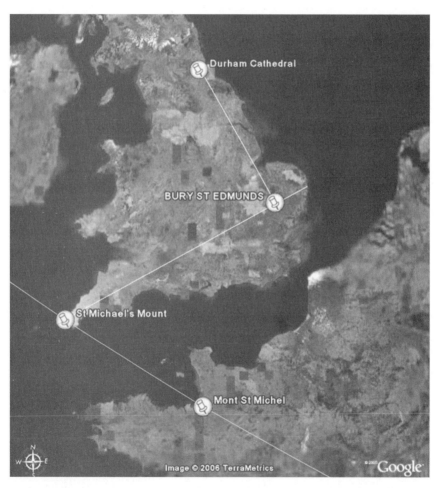

Figure 6.10. The right angle between the Michael Line and Durham Cathedral, where William established a combined secular and sacred bishopric and Benedictine Monastery.

St. Michel, south of its first practical use in Durham, soon after the Norman invasion. It indicates the strong role of the Normans in the development of the Gothic style.

The Norman relationship to the Benedictines is particularly intriguing, as it appears to have been a partnership with knowledge about the importance of ancient places. This type of knowledge corresponds exactly with what must have existed in megalithic times and was inherited by the pagan Celts and others who were sympathetic to the meaning of the landscapes in which they lived, the very cultures the Normans often suppressed. Thus, in our context of men from the north derived from a seafaring megalithic age, we are faced with the possibility that history may be guided by knowledge and intelligence that lies in the background as a question mark.

The ancient centers where the Benedictines sited cathedrals and churches were part of a megalithic network of sacred sites that had been organized upon the Earth, sometimes with a twelve-fold geometry. As we have seen, this creation of patterns of meaning is found in Norse lands. Add to this the ancient model of Earth, the widespread dispersion of weights and measures, and the numerical model of harmony based upon twelve, and it is hard *not* to see that there is a single phenomenon at work.

We should recognize that whoever developed and understood these systems came from a different civilization than the Medieval because the idea of energies aligned with points on Earth, special or sacred places, is deeply "pagan." It belongs to a category of ideas that became taboo in the very society that was honoring this knowledge by using it to guide the construction of grand edifices, to the glory of God!

Was this intentional? Taboos are created to contain energy, and a culture is probably delineated by its *taboo makers*. This certainly appears to have been the case with the Church in the Middle Ages: The re-use of ancient sacred sites and, as we have seen, the inner history that unwinds along the Apollo and Michael Lines is a continuum that bridges apparent discontinuities in the outer history of Europe. This phenomenon appears worthy of consideration.

SEVEN

ANGELS OF
THE TRANSFINITE

The archangel Michael and his lines present a very great enigma to a scientific age. The age of monotheistic religion that preceded modern science integrated Michael under the auspices of angelology, an area of belief close to pantheism, the belief in many gods. In essence, if the one God is in control, then his angels, fallen or not, come within his jurisdiction and hence are acceptable Works of God. Many an invaded ethnic group has used this sub-clause in the medieval Christian pantheon to translate their own divinities into saints or angels of the Church, having realized that the archetypes represented by Jesus Christ or the Virgin Mary were actually like the very archetypes they were being forced to denounce.

In fact the people of Rome adapted elements of pantheism into Christianity when Constantine was establishing the Roman Church. For instance, Christmas was dated four days after the winter solstice, which was traditionally the festival of the re-born Sun. As should now be clear, the Sun and planets are the origin of the gods of pantheism, whose characterizations were based upon their numerical and phenomenal characteristics. As such, they are the primary archetypes of a system of knowledge and not a pantheon of historical saints.

The word *archetype* is very much like the word *archangel*. If angels such as Michael were actually archetypes, then perhaps they had orig-inally been understood mathematically, like the gods who have been revealed to be planets with specific numerical relationships at their heart. If so, then the geometrical and numerical presentation and manifestation of the angel Michael could quite simply point to another unique way of dividing up reality. Such a characterization would make angels and archangels participants in the nature of the physical universe or, more specifically, in the creation of the spiritual landscape of Earth.

LOCATING THE WORLD OF SPIRITS

The genius mathematician Georg Cantor (creator of set theory, 1845–1918) recognized an important property of the same number "field," which, as chapter 2 demonstrated, generates harmony through its small-est numbers: The whole of the number field is uncountable and there-fore expresses the basic concept of infinity. Cantor realized that where there are a large number of objects in relationship to each other, as *the numbers themselves are,* and as *all the objects in the universe must also be,* then all of their relationships far exceed the number of objects them-selves. These relationships then become new but different uncountables that belong to a *set of infinites.*

Thus, some new types of number sets, greater than infinity, must exist, along with some way of signifying and even operating on them. He called the basic type of infinity, which is created by counting an infinite set, *Aleph Zero.* If all the different ways of grouping numbers were to be considered, they would be uncountable; he called this result *Aleph One,* since it was itself made up of many uncountable infinites. These new types of super numerical relationships—termed "transfinite" by Cantor—offer the possibility of understanding angels as unique operators or archetypes, with a unique mathematical core for each.[1]

J. G. Bennett became interested in the transfinite mathematics of Cantor because it explained a difference between two different worlds of experience, called by the Sufis the "World of Bodies" *(Aleph Zero)* and the "World of Spirits" *(Aleph One).* In other words, the spirit world could be made up of relationships within and between the whole systems, giving them transfinite characteristics.

The idea of grouping numbers used by Cantor is a familiar one. The Fibonacci series, for example, is one of many series that approximate the Golden Mean between successive elements.* The bodies of living organisms often hold this relationship between their key dimensions. The Golden Mean therefore would make a very good candidate for an archangel of life, especially considering that the Sun and Moon generate the proportion of the Golden Mean within the sky calendar. They further do so in harmony with the 1.6 year synod of Venus, who is associated with the Virgin Mother and her precedents.[2]

Wherever this relationship/proportion/ratio exists, the *spirit* of the Golden Mean could be said to exist. While there are an infinite number of ways of achieving this ratio, there is only one manifestation, *the ratio itself*. This could have inspired the thinking behind angels, especially in the construction of monuments and temples that needed to have an appropriate connection to objective reality within the numerical worldview.

In fact our acts of knowledge are themselves composite perceptions, so that similar relationships tend to have a name, as in "*that* is *a metaphor,*" meaning that all metaphorical statements belong to a single class that are identifiable and uniquely named as "metaphor." In this sense the World of Spirits is ever-present in the process of *making meaning* itself. But the direct connection can be lost, just as the dimensions of a building can have subliminal proportions that influence the aesthetic, irrespective of any understanding such as "this is a Golden Mean proportion."

This type of effect could well lie behind the idea of numerical enchantment at a sacred site. If relationships and proportions *are* manifestations of a spirit world, then the structuring of the landscape by ancient cultures is comprehensible as a spiritual technique. This provides

---

*In fact, any series where $X_{n+1} = X_n + X_{n-1}$ will tend toward the Golden Mean between successive members after a number of iterations; the Fibonacci series is just the exemplar for this property of blended sums.

important clues for the study of monuments, their measures, and the intended meaning of a given site.

Is it a coincidence, for instance, that the interrelation of number and function is especially clear within ancient metrology and musical harmony? When we look at the proportions used, they employ low prime number relationships, as if these were somehow the primary gods of proportion within the numbers below twelve (see chapter 2). However, musical proportions are different than the Golden Mean; musical intervals express the *cosmic order* found in pure musical tones, which is seen clearly in the Moon's relationships to the outer planets (a whole tone of 8:9 to Jupiter's synodic period and a half tone of 15:16 to Saturn's synodic period).

The Golden Mean belongs to a different class of numbers that are called "irrational," which means that they cannot be represented by any kind of simple fraction, involving one whole number over another whole number, no matter how large the numbers used are. Such numbers can generally only be approximated, either geometrically or through an *infinite mathematical series*. An irrational therefore represents not so much a number as a proportion or a function, which meets the criterion of belonging to *Aleph One* or the World of Spirits. In this respect they seem to naturally complement the ratios of musical harmony, rather like the demons that complement the gods in the Indian cosmological picture, *The Churning of the Ocean of Milk* (which can be seen as a depiction of the Pole and the Milky Way, fig. 7.1).

These irrational numbers relate to the realities of creation on the *surface of the planet* rather than in the *music of the spheres* that expresses the relatedness of Earth to the cosmos. New proportions might be expected within the creation of this new type of spherical world and its crust, with an all-important biosphere. If gods or archangels are to be found on Earth then they are likely to be identifiable as new proportions, both in the phenomena themselves and in human iconographies. Such angels could be associated with the irrational proportions found within sacred geometry.

A further clue is that the Golden Mean was built into many classical

Figure 7.1. The Churning of the Ocean of Milk, *a depiction of a precessional myth enacted by the gods and demons. (From Prasat Phnom Da, 12th century, Angkor Wat Style.)*

temples of the Bronze and Iron Ages where the Sun and *inner planets* (Mercury and Venus) were worshipped. The inner solar system represents a break with the simpler harmonies found in the outer planets because the inner planets are viewed from the moving platform of Earth while they revolve around the Sun. The Golden Mean is associated with the number five, living structures, the pentagram, and the planet Venus seen from Earth. It therefore seems likely that the spiritualizing force upon the *non-living* matter of Earth's crust is the number six, along with *hexagonal geometries* that can be related to Mercury.

MERCURY/HERMES AND THE CREATION OF SPACE

Coming into existence means the birth into and hence the creation of space. The surface of Earth is a creation of space *as we know it*. The planetary surface replaces the rotational systems of the solar system with three quite real dimensions, two horizontal (the horizon of local space) and one vertical (nadir and zenith). This requires gravity operating at the planetary surface. Life on the surface requires celestial and seasonal change. The daily Sun drives water between atmosphere, land, and sea to create primary erosion, while the monthly Moon drives the tides.

Hermes, whose name literally means "stone heap," is portrayed as the creator of the landscape spaces within which civilizations come and go. If Mercury *creates the landscape* then it is through crystalline geology and the moving around of material. The rocks themselves have a special energy to which human beings have a demonstrable sensitivity, as seen in dowsing. And these Earth energies also have a power to create space in the human imagination and make new things happen within cultures. So, what is space when we imagine it?

When we imagine a place, it is the power of the human mind to visualize space that becomes active. In other words, when we remember a scene from the past it is because we have *rebuilt the space* or at least our experience of it, with our senses. Our memory of places is also a conceptual power; we use spaces as symbols that can be manipulated. This is probably why Mercury was seen as the bringer of knowledge but also as a trickster, for this visual imagination is also capable of hallucination (knowing things that are not true) and the deception of others. Creation of spaces is therefore at the heart of *both planetary creation and of the human creative powers*. This subtle fact was implicit within traditional systems of knowledge where the brain was associated with Mercury, the messenger.

On many a medieval roof or chapel can be found the archangel Michael, who is associated therefore with the medieval network of Gothic cathedrals. It seems the cathedral network was related to him as being his work. In this a number of characteristics are constellated:

- Michael holds a golden sword, just as Mercury stands above the rising sun at dawn.
- The solar rays are a distinctive source of straight lines in nature, glancing over the land as if activating its creative potential, while the St. Michael and Apollo places (of chapter 5) are linked by straight lines often termed *leylines*.
- Like Mercury to the Sun, the archangel is closest to God and similarly conveys an *organizing idea* of divine hierarchy as a civilizing agency. He is pitted against the energies of Earth (portrayed as a dragon), and involved in a process of sanctifying places. In this way the alchemy of chaos leading to order on the surface of the planet is portrayed by Michael's weapon penetrating the body of the dragon.

As Earth came into existence, the surface had to develop many characteristics that raised it above the status of an unstructured rock. Great cycles of recycling had to take place to create a wealth of intermediate materials such as metamorphic and igneous rocks that eroded to make sand and clay, and to develop the necessary high surface areas for chemical and biochemical transfers. Thus the surface geology became activated for life. Mercury represents this transformation of raw thing into the useable materials for life.

As stated in chapter 1, Mercury has exactly three inferior and three superior conjunctions within the year, forming a hexad within the solar zodiac (fig. 7.2). This hexagon would have been familiar to Moses as the prime iconographic symbol of Thoth, the Egyptian Mercury, magician and measurer of Earth, who embodies the ancient accurate value of pi as 22/7 built into the ancient model of Earth (see chapter 3). The hexagon tessellates perfectly (covers a plane without overlapping or leaving gaps), which means that the number six is uniquely powerful in regard to the nature of three-dimensional space and the perfect filling of space.

Thus what we are seeing in the portrayal of the archangel Michael or Apollo is the planet Mercury as an archetype, and the Apollo-Michael

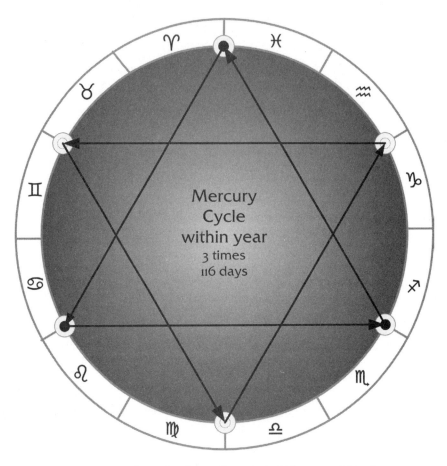

Figure 7.2. Star of David and synodic period of Mercury within the year.

Lines are part of the function of relatedness within physical space that gave Mercury the archaic designation of "guardian of the pathways" and, later on, patron of a European pilgrimage network.

The clues within the places along these lines are given in the cracking patterns of volcanic plugs, which are hexagonal columns, like those of the Giant's Causeway in Ireland. Such patterns do not emerge from the crystal structure of the rock as such, but arise due to the balanced forces acting upon the material as it contracts. Research on cracking patterns in drying concrete has revealed that isotropic or balanced stress causes *hexagonal patterns* to form, involving relative angles of 30°.

In his investigations of oracular connections[3] to the hexagon shape and other derivatives of root three, Robert Temple has found the hexagon in most surfaces, especially those in which there are energy transformations such as melting or freezing. The skin of the body is a set of flattened hexagon shapes, and cells in general use six-fold tubes as intercellular valves through their membranes. Earth's atmosphere often forms hexagonal convection cells, which are echoes of those created on the solar surface.

Mercury is deeply etched into the memory of the group soul. He is ever at work preparing the soil, by marking and demarking meaning within our landscapes. Thus he is prime enchanter and clearly the primary agent in the traditions of geomancy in the past, since his spirit both prepares and maintains the pathways of the soul within a given society. We know that within the world of human life, Mercury (as Hermes) became the divinity of boundaries and pathways in the landscape.

For the living and the dead, this *guardian of the threshold* mediates between the World of Bodies and the World of Spirits. He is the knower of the deep connections between places that have a secret power, a power sometimes associated with oracles that speak of the future and angels who interpret dreams, instruct prophets, or create an event that resonates on through human memory, informing the culture of its roots and destinations.

If the linking of places is a mercurial function and if Mercury is related to a six-fold nature, this suggests the origin of the twelve-fold patterns of the Indo-Europeans. Their interlinking of places considered sacred, traversing the landscape at multiples of 30° relative to northeast-south-west, is a sacred geometry based upon the two prime numbers two and three, which multiply to give six and twelve. Major oracles or other sacred functions were established at places on these lines, the most famous being the oracle at Delphi.

A view of the midsummer sunrise from Delphi looks directly over Athens to Delos, birthplace of Apollo, and beyond toward Mount Carmel on the Apollo Line that touches southern Britain. Between Greece and Crete lies latitude 36° where the *winter and summer sun rise exactly 30° south and north* of east and set similarly in the west (fig. 7.3).

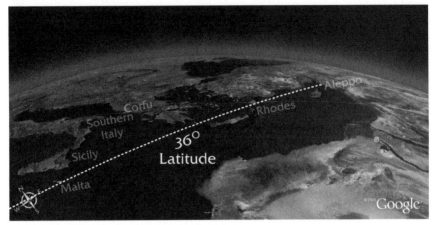

Figure 7.3. The Mediterranean and latitude 36° at which the solstice sunrise occurs exactly 30° north of east in midsummer and 30° south of east in midwinter.

To an ancient eye therefore, this latitude was significant as expressing the perfect location for twelve-fold centers. The Normans occupied much of this land at some stage, including western North Africa, Malta, Corfu, Rhodes, and Aleppo, as if drawn, consciously or unconsciously, to this latitude, just as they were to the Apollo and Michael Lines of northwest Europe.

SACRED GEOMETRICAL SPACES

The Mercurial geometry of the hexagon is a key to another powerful symbol, the Vesica Pisces, seen especially clearly in medieval building plans (fig 7.4). The key proportion is the square root of three, which is produced by a right angled triangle with a hypotenuse of two and a shortest side of one, for $2^2 - 1^2 = 3$. Two such triangles together form the equilateral triangle, two of which form the Star of David, six the hexagon, and so on. The tangent of this triangle is the square root of three and the acute angle is 30°, the angle of the Apollo-Michael Lines.

It is often remarked that the Vesica symbol could represent the vulva and as such harks back to the Earth Mother or the "gap between the worlds" in which something new can arise from the blending of Earth

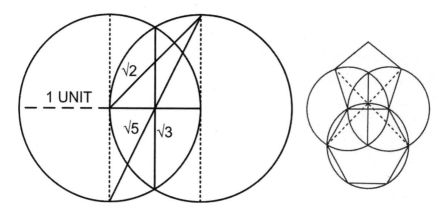

Figure 7.4. The Vesica Pisces. Made by two circles touching each other's center, this figure can generate three important irrational numbers belonging to the square ($\sqrt{2}$), the pentagon ($\sqrt{5}$), and the hexagon ($\sqrt{3}$). For this reason, the pentagon and hexagon are compatible.

and sky. The purpose for sacred building has to be that the building contributes in some way to what can happen within it. The conventional view is rather that sacred building techniques were purely symbolic, based upon traditions naturally lost without direct sources from those times. But if these sacred geometries operate from first principles—that geometry changes what people experience, or changes *how they think*—then such traditions might be self-evident within the buildings.

If Chartres affects people profoundly it seems highly likely that its unique building design is instrumental in this. Since the building was based upon pre-Christian traditions then the Church was employing these traditions subliminally exactly in the mode of the trickster Mercury, who is subliminal and "of the boundaries."

In the medieval period geometries based upon six suddenly became the organizing idea for all manner of sacred sites and buildings. The concept is a very simple one: This numerical archetype has an effect on how we feel and think. If true, the iconography behind gods and angels would have had its origin in the humanization of this idea of archetypal spaces and the sense of the sacred; slowly this became modern religion, where the numerical nature of the archetypes was veiled, if not lost altogether.

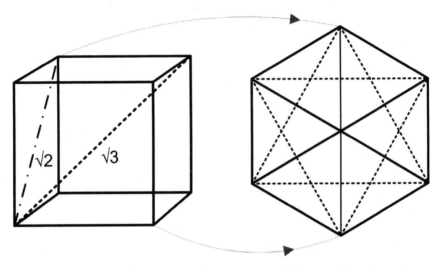

Figure 7.5. The unit cube generating the square root of three and its axiometric form as the hexagon.

The mythology of Apollo and Michael always refers to a reform of the previous matriarchal order, within sacred places such as Delphi. The female is veiled as a dragon or a serpent, as in the tale of Apollo killing python at Delphi. The dragon is usually eating women or maidens, often nine in number, since female priestesses* were often organized in groups of three or nine, three times three, a number associated with the Moon.[4] The lance of a heroic knight becomes equated with the straight rays of light from the Sun, penetrating Earth, the Goddess, exactly as the Church of God was eliminating the *explicit worship* of Earth and cosmos on behalf of the solar hero.

The Star of David, hexagon, equilateral triangle, and Vesica Pisces all embody the number three and the square root of three. The hexagon shape leads to the essence of the matter, for it is the shape formed by the edges of a cube when it is looked at from its longest axis, that is, with two opposite corners lined up (fig. 7.5).

This longest axis of a cube is equal to the square root of three in length, if the cube has edges one unit long. The only obvious religious

---

*The priestess of Apollo at Delphi who transmitted the oracles was called a Pythoness.

structure in the shape of a cube is the Kaaba at Mecca whose name means "cube" (fig. 7.6). But the prescription within religion for cubic rooms and altars comes at least from Greek and Jewish traditions:

- The Holy of Holies of Solomon's temple was defined as cubic in the Old Testament.
- The altar of Apollo on his island birthplace, Delos, was a cube.
- New Jerusalem was described as cubic in the *Book of Revelations*.

The cube is truly a space, whereas the hexagon is the flattening of the cube into two dimensions. However the hexagon retains the square root of three that is the signature of the three dimensions taken together as a cube. The hexagon apparently inherits its unique ability to fill space from the cube, along with the *passing of a measure* into two dimensions, onto a surface, the measure being the square root of three.

Cubes were also used to define the structures of the medieval cathedrals of Western Europe. The cathedrals adopted a new layout of internal pillars called the *ad triangulum* style based upon the square root of

Figure 7.6. The Kaaba circa 1900.

three flattened into two dimensions. The value of this square root is approximately 1.732 but—being irrational and unsuited to integer representation—it is used as the archetypal signature of Michael and Mercury. The famous Egyptian cubit, 1.728 feet long, is an approximation to the square root of three, its formula being $6^3/5^3$ or the cube of Mercury over Venus.

All of the three-based geometries were implicit in the construction of the cathedrals. The use of pillars and columns is a long tradition, seen in extreme form in Luxor, Egypt and forming the entire outer rectangle of the Parthenon in Athens, Greece. At the top of a column would generally be a lintel, an element seen in the Sarsen Circle of Stonehenge. For load-bearing a lintel is limited by its brute strength to resist the forces caused by building on top of it. The Romanesque tradition developed the circular arch to provide the strength to hold up greater weights, though its weakness lay exactly in the middle where, like a lintel, it was horizontal.

The Gothic adopted the pointed arch design from the Islamic world, which is often called a Gothic arch. Its primordial form is exactly the Vesica Pisces, in which two circles touch each other's centers. It contains the square root of three, width to height, but other types of pointed arch result if the centers of the circles are placed closer to each other until, when the centers coincide, a circle is produced (fig. 7.7).

To make arches other than the Vesica, therefore, an odd number of divisions are defined. With five divisions, a "one fifth" arch is made by using points two and three as the centers for two arcs. In this way an arch can be made sharp enough to suit any width of opening while maintaining the geometrical theme within the whole building.

Less visible than the Gothic arches of the cathedrals is the network of equilateral triangles initiated at the "crossing," which lies in the heart of a Gothic church, found where the long body of the church *crosses* the transepts on either side (ignoring any of the side aisles of these elements).[5] The whole plan of Chartres is based upon its crossing. If the crossing is one unit across the minor axis, then the central eight columns define a length of root three. From this center, a pattern is created

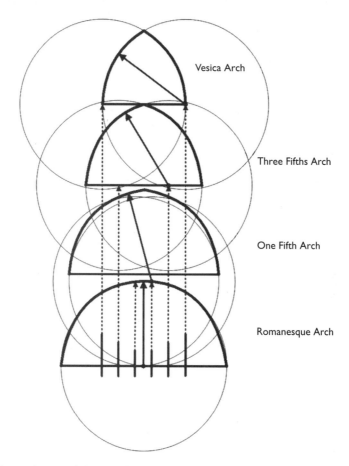

Figure 7.7. The evolution of the arch from Romanesque through the Gothic to the pure Vesica.

upon which the cathedral design can be developed using only the points defined by an expanding *ad triangulum* grid. Thus, while variety was possible, the rule of root three was always a *foundation stone* in such designs (fig. 7.8).

The Romanesque style that preceded the Gothic had been based upon the idea of harmony between whole number ratios. The result was circular arches and *ad rectangulum,* the use of whole number rectangles. At Chartres, the Gothic cathedral was built on the site of a Romanesque cathedral that had burned down in the last of a series of fires. It is quite likely, as we see in the next chapter, that the first Gothic churches were

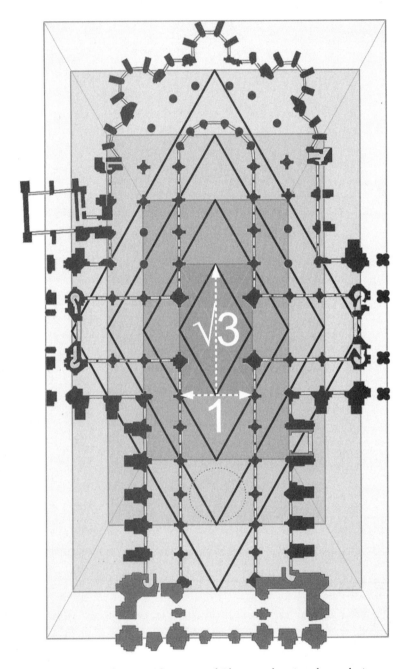

√3

1

Figure 7.8. The ground pattern of Chartres showing the evolution of the √3 proportion from within the layout of the crossing. (After Gordon Strachan, Chartres: Sacred Geometry, Sacred Space [Edinburgh, Scotland: Floris Books, 2003].)

adapted Romanesque churches, and that the new feature was primarily the incorporation of the square root of three.

As a floor plan, therefore, the new Gothic cathedral design drew an ever-expanding vulva upon the horizontal Earth, to represent on its surface the same power of Mercury-Michael that prepares Earth's crust as a sacred space. The square root of three also defines the structure in the vertical up to the arched vault which has the form of the Gothic pointed shape (fig. 7.9). At Chartres the vault is defined as an arch by the pentagon, with all its Golden Mean relationships and association with Venus as Virgin. Extending the archetypal metaphor in this way, the vertical

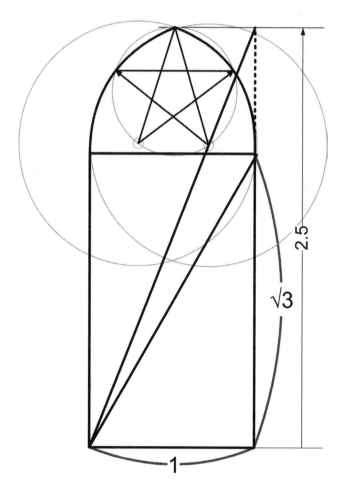

Figure 7.9. Vertical use of root three at Chartres.

dimension indicates life emerging triumphantly out of the soil prepared by Michael's "ploughing" of the surface.

These buildings were placed upon the ancient places not just to overlay their pagan precursors but also to employ the same Earth energies in the service of God, by the sign of the dragon-slayer. Also achieved was the creation of an archetypal space that combines the essence of the inner planets' numerical characteristics. This has been called "objective art" in that it connects to meaning in such a way that the transfinite could be grasped through the vehicle of the human, evolved, imagination of space.

Below the floor lie the chthonic spaces of Earth Goddess, still present as prehistoric or pre-medieval crypt spaces, suited to the Black Madonna, and ancient healing wells. The vertical has been transformed therefore between the underworld of the oracular and womb-like to the raised pentagon where the female has become entirely conceptual and celestial as Venus.

The esoteric story and the symbolic production are therefore alternative tracks, the former only for the initiate to the mysteries in question. The breaks in history and more broadly, between prehistory and the present, are an illusion affecting only those caught up in existential affairs. The symbols have not changed that much, even though the names have. The religious architecture is still wrapped up in archetypes connected with the sky and the fundamental differentiations of space found in ancient sacred geometry.

THE PATTERN OF TROY

One of the inexplicable additions to many a cathedral floor was the labyrinth. Many of these were removed during the French Revolution but perhaps the greatest still remains on the floor of Chartres cathedral. Between the cathedral's twin towers to the Sun and the Moon lies the famous Rose Window. Were this wall to fall intact onto the cathedral floor, the Rose Window would cover exactly the circle within which the labyrinth is drawn.

We will look more deeply into the design of Chartres in the next chapter, but the labyrinth gives, by its position, a simple key to the whole. A circle centered in the midst of the crossing, the central focus of a Gothic church, passing through the center of the labyrinth, also passes through the center of the apse or rond point at the end of the choir. In other words, there is a perfect symmetry of these three centers expressed in figure 7.10 by three circles, each passing through another's center point. The labyrinth and the apse represent the two ends of the Romanesque church upon which the Gothic edifice was built, the foundations of which became the lower levels of the present cathedral. It appears that the crossing was placed exactly between the two ends of the old church.

A labyrinth is not a maze, as there is only *one route* into its center and the same therefore to leave it. It has been compared with the concept of coming into this world and leaving it again, through the spheres of planetary influence. At a more practical level, pilgrims considered traversing it a spiritual blessing and pilgrimage in itself (fig. 7.11).

The labyrinth at Chartres was based upon eleven levels while another very familiar pattern, the Cretan labyrinth, is based upon seven levels. Both relate to the natural labyrinth of the intestines, which were used widely in the ancient world as oracles for divination (fig. 7.12). As with the labyrinth, there is only one path through the intestines, which were considered to be a mirror of the cosmos. Here again the intestinal god is associated with Mercury, while the layers of a labyrinth represented, in the intestine and labyrinth alike, planetary levels and hence the solar system. As the knowledge of the intestinal god and the oracular network of sacred places were both linked to Mercury, finding such a symbol on the floor of medieval cathedrals indicates a pure continuity of tradition.

The seven-fold labyrinth pattern—often called "Troy" or "Troy Town"—has been shown mathematically unique as the best natural design. This could explain its existence within many areas of the world. In northwest Europe labyrinths of this pattern have been found from Scandinavia to Ireland. In the Americas the Hopi Indians had a version,

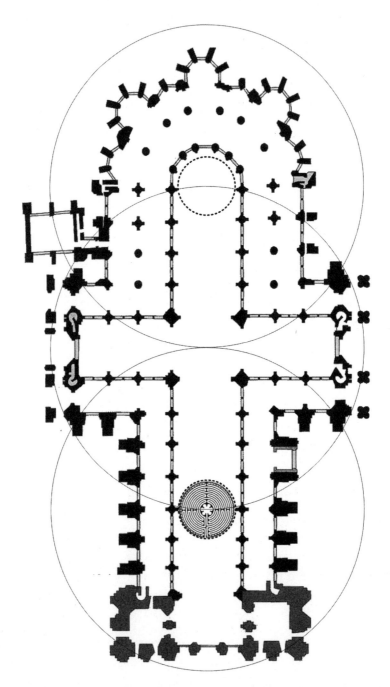

Figure 7.10. The two centers of apse and labyrinth define the ends of the previous Romanesque church. The new crossing of the Gothic appears to have been placed exactly between the two.

Figure 7.11. The eleven-fold labyrinth of Chartres.

Figure 7.12. The intestinal god was associated with augury performed on entrails, the main reason for animal sacrifice, which was an attempt to see the future through patterns arising in nature. Humbaba, circa 7th century B.C.E. (British Museum).

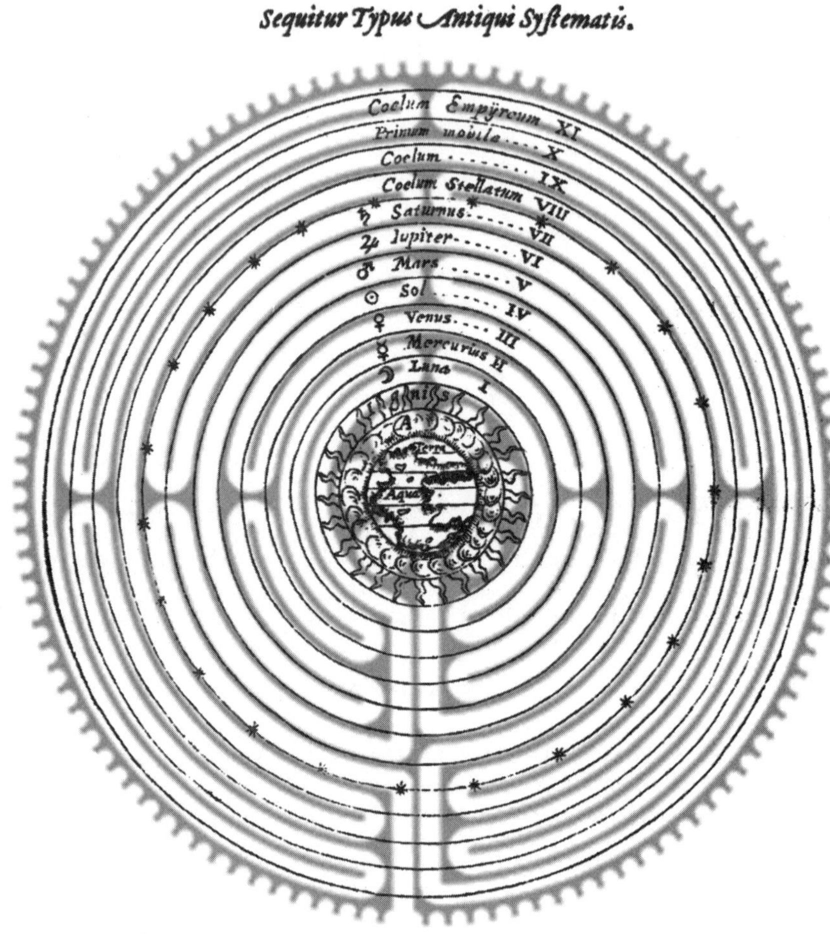

Figure 7.13. Aristotle's worldview as Critchlow's interpretation of the labyrinth found at Chartres. (After Keith Critchlow et al., "Chartres Maze, a model of the universe?," RILKO Occasional Paper No 1.)

while the earliest datable ones are in Galacia, northwest Spain (c. 2500–1800 B.C.E.), and on the back of a Linear B tablet from a Mycenaean palace at Pylos in southern Greece (c. 1200 B.C.E.).

One theory about the labyrinths' possible significance is that they were the sign of a ritual for *establishing a new center,* which was achieved by coming into the center by a circuitous route. The idea of eleven layers to be navigated is implied in Aristotle's worldview of the four spheres beyond the planets, and seven planetary spheres (making eleven). The smaller labyrinth design of seven perhaps represents just the planets. Keith Critchlow, using the medieval Aristotelian model, has interpreted the eleven layers found at Chartres as *the way in and out of the planetary system* with Earth at the center.

EIGHT

THE TEMPLE'S LAST STAND

A culture or civilization is defined by what is *in* and what is *out*. The simple version of *out* is whatever is beyond the geographical or cultural borders of the empire. Some cultural components, while *out*, may from time to time be reviewed and then tolerated or have to be removed. The pre-classical corpus we have called "Atlantis" still existed around the time of Christ through many forms of belief and the different ethnic groups that held them. Thus, a tapestry of culture lay beneath, for example, the Roman Empire, whose main interest was the taxation of its great empire.

As Christianity was incorporated into the pagan religious life of Romans by Constantine the Great (272–337), the interaction with the land and sky so important to ancient religion was replaced by the power of the *Word:* interaction with language and the mind itself. It was as if an *Age of Ideas* was in the ascendant. This trend had been born in the form of Greek philosophical speculation and technical innovation, even though philosophers were still intimidated and threatened if and when their ideas were perceived as *disrespectful to the gods.*

While this Greek movement of philosophy was detached from religion, it eventually merged with the religion of Jesus. This was effected by the strong cultural impact of the Greek speaking world upon the eastern Mediterranean, through its powerful center at Alexandria, and later, through the Roman intellectual life that was modeled on classical Greek pantheism. The most Greek of the four gospels, *The Gospel of John,* opens with the declaration: "In the beginning was the Word, and the Word was with God, and the Word was God." Word in Greek is *Logos,* a primordial whole within which all intelligibility was contained, that is, all the meaning latent in the mind of God.

The Logos presented an alternative source of meaning to that of the numerical worldview, or at least it was construed from it that the *philosophical categories* generated by the Greek philosophers were in some sense real but within a *landscape of the mind* rather than in the *ancient sacred landscapes* of Earth. The wordy alternative to numbers formed the basis for the new *mental* worldview seen in neo-Platonist thought. Plato himself stands between the prehistoric and new thinking just like the apocalyptic angel of *Revelations,* with one foot on *numeric creationism* and the other on *mental creationism.*

Yet the *Word emanating from God* is very similar to the physical arrangements found in the inner solar system, and hence of the Sun god and his immediate family of Mercury and Venus. Indeed, Mercury is thought to be the source of language itself, a fact very compatible with his trickster nature since words can be wise or deceptive. Classical culture was a pantheistic system based upon a solar pantheon, somehow animated by Zeus-Jupiter who had deposed Chronos/Saturn, the god of time. Saturn had himself deposed a previous ruler Uranos by cutting off this sky god's genitals. According to the myth, Aphrodite Venus arose from where they dropped. She was formed "out of the foam of the sea," that is, she emerged out of the foam of sunset and sunrise, as first the evening and then the morning star. As the divine messenger, Mercury dashes about the solar deity on his winged feet, to form a "burning bush" or, more systematically, the Star of David.

At the very least Greek philosophy and Jewish monotheism had been integrated into Christianity by the time fourth century Romans were able to embrace it without persecution. Arguably, other components from the ancient world were held within the Jewish system of thought, such as Egyptian and Chaldean knowledge of metrology—witness the sacred rod of the Jews and the seven day week.

The progress of monotheism and of Word-based religions can be seen as the progress of the idea of history as well, since the recording of events creates a wordy world of meaning. This led to a further synthesis: that the emergence of history was the story of God and his battle against forces that would deny his supremacy. This is a myth-making function that lies behind the authorization of empire builders and in this can be seen its utility for the mutually supportive church and state in the feudal medieval age.

Storytelling became a history that continued through Europe's Dark Ages to the medieval period. The latter was both a flowering and freezing over of some new ideas. The medieval culture left in its wake a wealth of newly styled buildings that seem to incorporate the ancient arts of number, yet it was dominated by a Roman Church that outwardly denied the ancient sense of the traditional arts except to its own specialist cadres. A tradition of underground secret societies became established, official and unofficial, which exists to this day. These societies, within the Church or outside it, often had a peculiar propensity for the old numerical arts and obsessive interest in the ancient world.

OF EMPIRES AND CRUSADES

Hitler's self-declared *Third Reich* referred to the two Roman Empires that dominated the first millennium, the Roman Empire and the Holy Roman Empire. The first was brought down by its internal corruption and a growing weakness in the face of mounted warrior nations to the north and east of its borders. Their presence was the product of migrations due to the worsening climate of the north, the slow end of the climatic optimum. Their descent into the Mediterranean was as inevitable as the entry of the Greeks had been more than a millennium earlier, and that of the Indians and Persians even further back (fig. 8.1).

The time frame of 300–900 C.E.—during which human migration occurred in the area that comprises central Europe—has been named "The Migration Period" by historians. The migration, which included

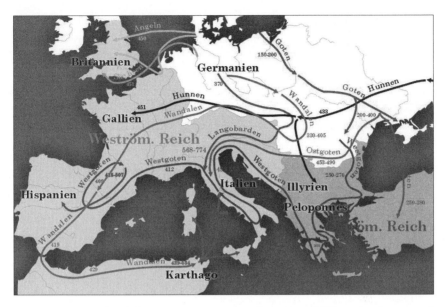

Figure 8.1. Second to fifth century migrations. (Courtesy of Wikimedia Commons.)

the Goths, Vandals, and Franks, among other Germanic and Slavic tribes, was a composite product of incursions by the Huns, population pressures, and climate change. The Romans were brought down by an alliance of the Vandals and the Visigoths, who had been converted to Christianity while living by the Black Sea in Dacia, modern-day Bulgaria. Their bishop Ulfilas (311–382) translated the gospels into their language, creating a Visigoth script in the process.

The Visigoths then became a policing ally for the new Roman Empire of the western Mediterranean, where they were used against the Vandals. Their reward came through their conquests of Spain and southern France, which became the Visigoth Kingdom (fig. 8.2). However the Visigoths had been converted to a non-Roman Christianity called Arianism in which Jesus, while divine, was nonetheless believed to have been created by God and was, consequently, inferior to him.* Rome thus associated the area between Spain and France with *heretical* thinking

---

*In Roman Catholicism, Arianism was denounced in 321 by the Council of Nicea, which asserted: "We believe in the Holy Spirit," and later, "and the Son," that is, the divinity of Christ and the Trinity.

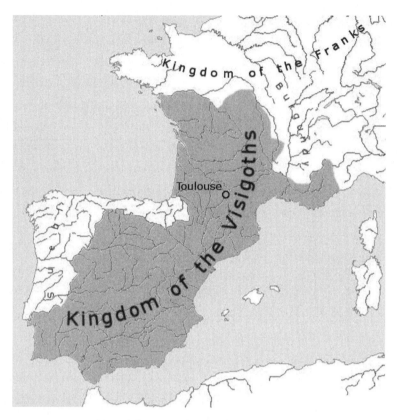

Figure 8.2. Kingdom of the Visigoths. (Courtesy of Wikimedia Commons.)

imported from Bulgaria, which later manifested in the medieval crusade against the Gnostic Cathars.

In 711 the Islamic Moors invaded Visigoth Spain from North Africa, and ruled most of Spain until the *reconquista* removed them from central Spain in 1212. The Moors had attempted to push beyond the Pyrenees until they were defeated by the Frankish war leader Charles Martel in 732. This victory was consolidated by the newly unified Frankish Kingdom under Charlemagne the Great (ca. 745–814), who was made emperor of the Holy Roman Empire in 800, which created the *Second Reich*.

Charlemagne had saved the Vatican in 774 from the Lombards (yet more Scandinavians who had occupied northern Italy around Milan). Like many other Scandinavian peoples they worshipped Earth Mother

Nerthus. After their defeat the Papal States were created, consolidating papal power. Although Charlemagne created a vast swathe of empire in western Europe, he did not take Spain from the Moors. The Muslim world remained a threat for many Christian territories, especially the Eastern Empire of Orthodox Christianity, and this explains the idea of the First Crusade.

In 1095 Pope Urban II called upon all Christians to join a war against the Turks in return for *full penance:* full forgiveness of their sins (including those committed in the Crusade). Jerusalem was taken in 1099, and the whole population was massacred, regardless of their religious faith, *even the indigenous Christians.*

The Crusade created an external enemy and caused the various feudal levels within Europe to fight less among themselves. It also created a precedent for the Church as spiritual overseer of secular powers through *canon law,* which included laws governing the aristocracy. As with the creation of the Papal States by Charlemagne, several small Crusader States were then created around a Kingdom of Jerusalem.

Before the Crusade, a highly influential transformation of the Benedictine order of monks had been initiated, carried forward, and exemplified by Bernard of Clairvaux (1090–1153). The transformation resulted in a new order of monks called the Cistercians. They reverted to the original Rule of St. Benedict, which had become somewhat diluted through, for instance, the elimination of manual work. Bernard reinstated this work, which raised the self-sufficiency and economic power of the monasteries, allowing them to reproduce, to create daughter houses. This rapidly created a network that soon covered western Europe with Cistercian houses, which would have been perfect for geodetic activities.

At the same time, a great deal of information became available from the Muslim world, which had been lost to the West since the decline of classical Rome. It was written in Arabic, Greek, Hebrew, and other languages, but largely comprised the works of classical antiquity. Aristotle and Plato were available in Arabic but in need of translation. While open centers of learning existed, particularly in Moorish Spain, translation services within Christendom were performed in monastic scriptoriums, which had specialists in biblical languages.

While the First Crusade took Jerusalem, Bernard's house of Burgundy and the house of Champagne were conspiring to set up a more radical religious organization—the *Knights Templar*. Outwardly their remit was to protect the routes and traffic to and from the Holy Land. Their immediate instructions, however, led them to become the *sole occupants* of the Temple Mount, the past location of Solomon's Temple, hence their given name of "the Poor Knights of Christ and of the Temple of Solomon."

For nine years just nine knights did little else to outward view other than occupy the Rock of Jerusalem. Historical research implies that the noble families in question had set up Bernard and his two orders to specifically recover items hidden below the former temple site, the so-called stables of Solomon. While speculation concerning every type of booty (the Ark of the Covenant, the Holy Grail, and so on) has become a popular pastime, it is most likely that they excavated a mixed cache, as documented in the Copper Scroll found as part of the Dead Sea Scrolls.

The problem with many of the documents belonging to the time before and just after the life of Christ is that they contradict the accepted history relied on by the Roman Church to support various claims within its creed. More ancient information, including details of ancient monument design rules, metrological standards, and geomantic techniques was also likely to have been represented. It seems quite clear from their presence at Michael/Apollo sites that the Benedictines already had some knowledge of geomancy and probably of other ancient sciences too. Early Cistercian establishments followed suit in "finding the right spot." Bernard thought only priests and monks should employ the traditional arts, despite the fact that masons and their guilds had caught hold of elements of them. The initial mission of the Knights Templar orders appears then to have been to recover lost and esoteric information, and to maintain its privileged use by the special orders.

THE EVOLUTION OF GOTHIC
CATHEDRAL DESIGN

Were Bernard of Clairvaux, and his Cistercian and Knights Templar orders, possessed of some new and secret knowledge, obtained perhaps from the Holy Land? Certainly, a myth has grown up suggesting that the Gothic was manifestation of this secret knowledge. There are many books cataloguing elements of the traditional arts, notably sacred geometry, with regard to Gothic cathedrals, especially that of Chartres, which is considered exemplary (fig. 8.3). But can a creational sequence be found that relates to Bernard, who spoke little of geometry within his voluminous writings? While Bernard was a highly influential figure in his time, the building of cathedrals after his death has become a puzzle because the connection between their construction and any secret knowledge shows little period of development and scant mention in the works of the time. Yet the depth and perfection of the resulting application of the traditional arts is surprising, since these arts were essentially not Christian. Rather they were projected into Christianity from traditional sources to form what came to be called the "Gothic" style.

While Gothic might have been a medieval slur, implying barbarous, it may also speak of the horsemen from the north who were consistently full of surprises and influence. After all, Bernard's people, the Burgundians, and his colleagues from Champagne had all been such when migrating from northern Germany and the Baltic in preceding ages.

Part of the answer to this question can be found in the pamphlet, *L'acoustique cistercienne et l'unité sonore* by Hubert Larcher, which details the philosophy used by Bernard in creating a series of chapels that are highly valued to this day for their exceptional acoustics, most famously those of Fontenay and Thoronet. They were employed primarily for Cistercian chant, which is a strict form of Gregorian and Benedictine chanting. Unlike the vast spaces of the later cathedrals, these spaces resembled the dark barrel-roofed churches found in Burgundy,

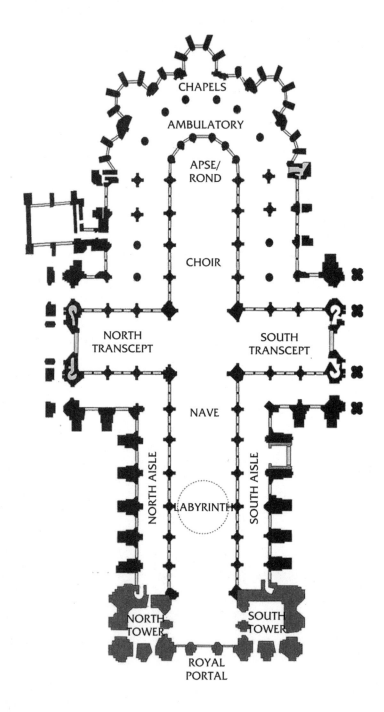

Figure 8.3. Traditional layout of a cathedral (Chartres).

transformed by the incorporation of the Golden Mean, in which "every note should have equal voice."

Robert Chalavoux has analyzed Bernard's last chapel, Thoronet, near Marseilles, for its sacred geometrical content. With regard to the Golden Mean, a number of repeated cells using this dimension are to be found, forming a rudimentary nave and aisles of four cells by four, to create a fundamental Golden Mean rectangle. Two more cells are added to form rudimentary transepts, largely for access (fig. 8.4).

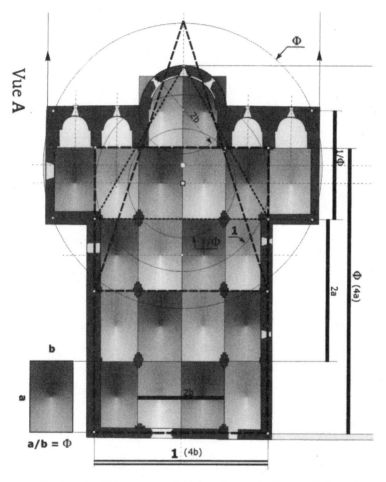

Figure 8.4. The church of Thoronet and the number of the Sun analysis and diagram kindly supplied by Robert Chalavoux. (From L'acoustique cistercienne et l'unité sonore *by Hubert Larcher, illustrated by Robert Chalavoux.)*

Also present in this church is a vestigial, circular apse from the very point of which Chalavoux draws an equilateral triangle, which may be a clue to the evolution into the Gothic. As we have seen, it is the crossing of the Gothic cathedral that differs from that of the Romanesque style. It incorporates the square root of three, one manifestation of which is the equilateral triangle. Before the crossing is the nave, where the congregation gathers, while beyond is the choir representing the most sacred space, generally to the east.

Thoronet has a nave but the choir is just a circular apse for the altar and the transepts are small and functional, forming a Tau cross rather than the conventional cross; this was the norm for Romanesque designs and for the earlier Chartres. On either side of the main altar are two smaller alcoves, making five in all.

Looking for musical ratios at Chartres immediately reveals that the main body of the cathedral can be defined by the ratio 15:16, the half tone, while the transept has a ratio defined by 8:9, the whole tone (fig. 8.5). The reader should remember from chapter 1 that these are the ratios of the Saturn and Jupiter synods to the lunar year. Both of these ratios are *to the same scale,* meaning that they apply acoustically within the church to the same frequency of standing wave, about eight times the height of the crossing height of forty-eight Roman feet, giving an infrasound standing wave frequency of 3 Hz—quite subliminal.

If the Thoronet plan is laid beneath a plan of Chartres, then the two are shown to differ by about one *foot* in Thoronet to one *pace,* of 2½ feet, in the Chartres design (fig. 8.6). The side aisles of Thoronet are in fact narrower than half the (double width) nave and match perfectly the aisles of Chartres. *The ratio of nave to side aisle is therefore giving rise to the ratio of the crossing.*

The four subsidiary alcoves at Thoronet become the double aisles of the ambulatory, which surrounds the choir. The choir of Chartres is based exactly on the Thoronet apse or central alcove, which has been projected forward to form the choir. While the three windows of the original altar space appear carried forward into the three main chapels belonging to the expanded apse of the Chartres design, they were in fact

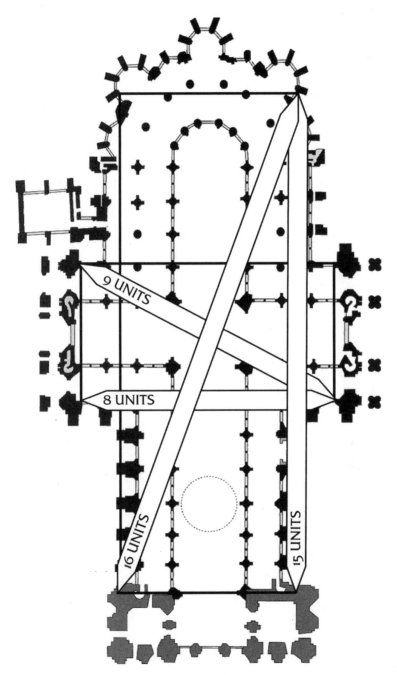

9 UNITS

8 UNITS

16 UNITS

15 UNITS

Figure 8.5. At Chartres the half and whole tone define the main body to transept dimension. This creates a major characteristic of the cathedral, its diminutive transepts.

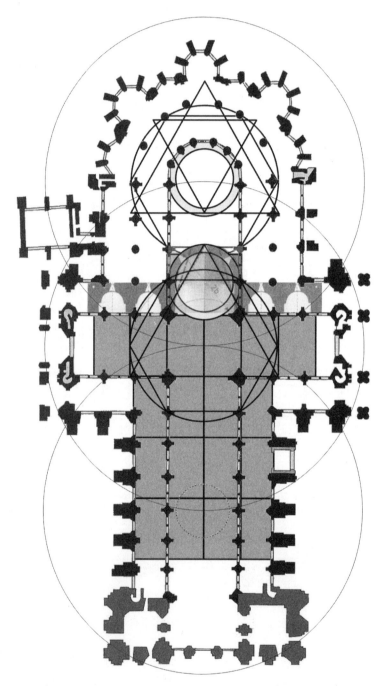

Figure 8.6. Combined floor plan of Thoronet (× 5/2) and Chartres

preexisting in the previous Romanesque church. In *Chartres* by Gordon Strachan, the front illustration very usefully shows the different churches on the Chartres site in plan, one upon another. This shows Thoronet to be a hybrid transition between Romanesque and Gothic and hence an actual stepping stone for that period of transition.

The basic cell size measured by Chalavoux at Thoronet was A = 8.37 meters and B = 5.18 meters. This makes B almost exactly 17 feet in length (16.995) and dividing by 13 and multiplying by 21 yields 27.46154 instead of the 27.46063 feet of A.* Thus Thoronet could have been efficiently designed using English feet and a 21/13 approximation to the Golden Mean.

What type of foot might have been employed at Chartres? John James associated the Roman foot with Chartres in *The Master Masons of Chartres*. He used a figure that was 6.8 feet to seven Roman feet, but this would not belong to ancient metrology, for its formula would then contain the prime number seventeen. The nearest of Neal's values would be the *root geographical Roman foot* where the root value of 24/25 feet is increased twice by 176/175 to give 0.971003 feet, a difference of less than 0.04 percent. James measured the crossing to be fifty-six feet by forty-eight feet, with a ratio of seven to six and a common unit of eight feet. Fifty-six feet is then the side length of the hexagon associated with the crossing and hence is also the radius of the circumscribing circle.

The total height of the hexagon is fifty-six times the square root of three ($\sqrt{3}$ = 1.7320508 . . .), which is effectively ninety-seven feet. Subtracting forty-eight from this and dividing by two gives the aisle width of 24.5 Roman feet. The masons would have been able to use such rational numbers only because fifty-six times $\sqrt{3}$ is ninety-seven or, more simply, $\sqrt{3} \approx 97/56 = 1.7321429$.

This shows how providential numerical devices can avoid the need for geometrical constructions when extending a ground plan. Similar

---

*The unit defined by the 21/13 relationship is very close to 9/8 of the standard reciprocal Persian foot.

shortcuts exist within the metrological grid in which 11/7 is manipulated to allow a rational number of slightly different feet in the diameter and radius of a circular structure. The choice of module, or type of foot, emerges naturally from the size of the level space available and the extent of the given design.*

Most of the remaining details of the construction at Chartres are visibly derived from the Thoronet and similar designs that existed in the lifetime of Bernard of Clairvaux. This contradicts the doctrine that Bishop Denis Sugar in Paris, plus Oriental and Norman influences, were generating a Gothic movement to which Bernard was opposed. It is perhaps more appropriate to say that Bernard and the Cistercians were purists and that for their needs a "small recording studio" was more appropriate than the large Gothic "concert halls" of the later cathedrals.

More important is the fact that the cathedrals were built on the old megalithic sites and that they embodied sacred geometrical patterns that have no explicit place in the religion of Jesus. It was the Arabs, Jews, and Greeks who expressed explicit numerical and geometrical knowledge in both their writings and buildings. In this respect, the myth that the Knight's Templar recovered lost and secret knowledge from beneath the Temple Mount in Jerusalem might point to the fact that the Gothic revolution had just such alien elements within its innovations, reapplied to the creation of a powerful new form of Christianity in the Middle Ages.

A beautiful iconography of the geometer's guild has possibly been found in the *Tarot of Marseilles* by Robert Vincent and Philippe Camoin. While the phenomenon of Tarot came centuries later, it appears that a piece of the geometer's art was placed in the card Valet du Baton—the knave of clubs (fig. 8.7). It ties together the Fibonacci Golden Mean and

---

*John Neal has shown this to be the case with the Iron Age brochs of northern Britain; they display rational internal diameters using most of the different types of foot measurements to achieve a desired size. The historical precedents of these measures belong, according to official history, thousands of miles distant from each other and thousands of years after the brochs were built. The broch builders must have known of the full set of ancient measures, easily derived from a single reference length, because all of them were rational fractions of the English foot.

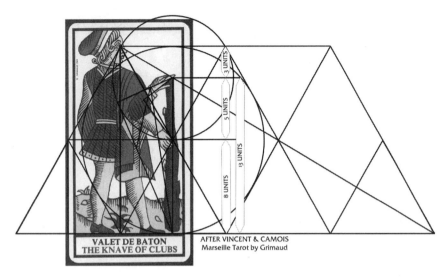

Figure 8.7. Valet de Baton from the Marseille Tarot.

√3 through sightlines at 30° and 60°. At one point the two sightlines generate a separation that contains the Golden Mean between them and the ground.

The same geometry can be used on the cathedral ground plan, as shown in figure 8.8.

The figure itself draws on a style of drawing from the ancient world, particularly of Egyptian temple art, deeply iconographic and having an underlying canon of proportion. It is not far different from the picture of Thoth within the hexagon and draws on the same 30° geometry. A tradition of building in stone would, over millennia, have naturally generated many rules of thumb, shortcuts, and stock solutions to geometric problems. This tarot card is extremely suggestive of one of these. The association with Marseilles thereafter appears to leave a clue that this cargo of know-how had passed through that port, which was the primary conduit for Templar logistics in the Mediterranean. The overall content of the Tarot, its possible connection with the Templars, and the origins of such a system of iconic knowledge (in northern Italy and the Languedoc) deserve more study.

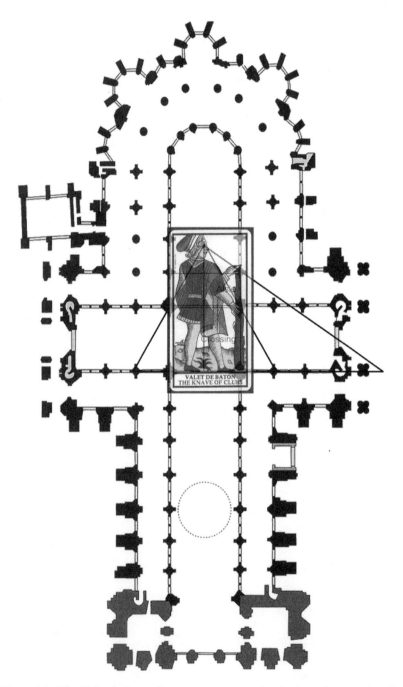

Figure 8.8. The Valet de Baton locating crossing and aisle. It is pleasing though romantic to see this figure as representing the guilds that built Chartres and the other Gothic cathedrals.

ANOTHER KIND OF WORSHIP

On a visit to the last Cathar stronghold of Montsegur in the Pyrenees I came upon a geometrical template of the castle on a postcard! It implied methodologies similar to sacred geometry when it was built, but when was it built? After the Crusaders took the castle, it was supposedly "shaved," that is, razed to the ground. However the new Monsignor for Montsegur, appointed by the king, is unlikely to have actually destroyed it, not least because a castle is built into its bedrock—destroying it is pointless if the castle is to continue.

If this is the case, then the castle remains as it was when the Cathars had it. Although they did not own castles, they had noble sympathizers who represented them in the world. That the castle was geometrical might imply that its builders came from a tradition conversant with a sacred building tradition, but which tradition might this be?

It is said of Montsegur that at summer solstice the rising sun shines

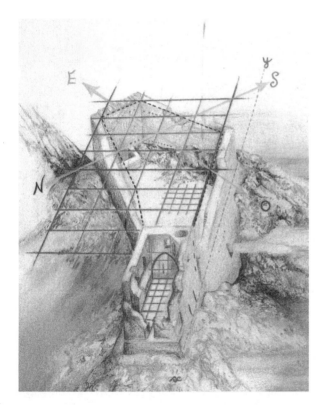

Figure 8.9. Postcard from Montsegur showing a design grid proposed by a previous guide to the monument, Patrick Garnier. (Reproduced with permission of the artist Yan Christine.)

just between two opposing arrow slits of the keep. As in figure 8.10, the chamfered sides of the two slits run at the angle of sunrise while the slits themselves are staggered in a way that creates a sunrise alignment. This keep and one wall of the castle run exactly northwest, making the castle subtly aligned to the cardinal directions but at forty-five degrees.

The shape of a castle has to take the opportunities offered by the pedestal of rock in question. Montsegur demonstrates that one could still define phenomena that do not align with the main axis of available space by using a cross alignment as between the staggered arrow slits. The longer the alignment the greater the accuracy of the resulting sighting line across the monument.

Ferdinand Neil has shown that a number of significant sightlines are

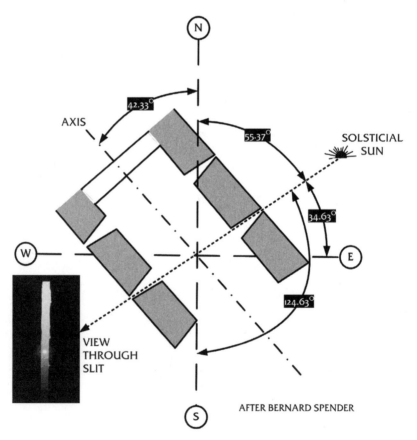

Figure 8.10. How the arrow slits of the keep at Montsegur are aligned to the summer solstice sunrise. (After the work of Bernard Spender and Ferdinand Neil.)

possible to enable the year and hence the zodiac to be annotated within the monument by sightings to the sun's position, primarily in the northwest but with possible sightings to the east and south also. This has caused the usual outcry that the monument is being over-interpreted by the occult-minded, outside of the academic community. However, somebody must have created these unusual alignments, at least of the whole structure forty-five degrees to the cardinal directions. The presence of short alignments is usually accompanied with those to the horizon, for on a mountain sanctuary the population naturally uses the horizon as a solar calendar: The mountain does not move and there are many distant landmarks.

The alignment of a dolman to solsticial sunrise thousands of years ago is a permitted norm but heretical Christians building a medieval monument with megalithic accessories is not. However, if the Cathars incorporated such practices, their beliefs might have been a form of dualism from the megalithic, since it is not known what religious systems had been developed in the megalithic.

The Cathars are thought to have come from Bulgaria, via Serbia as the Bogomils. Bulgaria was also the land of the Visigoths before their defeat of Rome. It is on the Black Sea and at the end of the swathe of Eurasian steppe lands, where Persian dualism (two gods, of good and evil, light and dark) had leaked into (or was indigenous to) the steppe tribes of Indo-European origin. The innovation of monotheism through the covert worship of the Sun god as Jehovah had created a completely different framework of belief in which evil was not a force of darkness but rather the rebellion of Lucifer, all having been created by one God.

The built spaces created by monotheism in the Middle Ages were interior, unlike the ancient sacred spaces oriented to the exterior alternation of light and darkness. The alignment of Chartres to the midsummer solstice represents a hangover from the pagan site, which was reused by monotheist builders. The attunement to light and dark was replaced by the worship of an interior space created by God, or at least the archangel Michael, and the "new Heaven and new Earth" were mental rather than environmental.

The Neo-Platonists of both the early and medieval Church considered mental objects as divine creations, real in themselves and having qualities that "emanated" from the Divine. Mercury is the perfect exemplar of this mental creationism: he was both close to the Sun, as well as being the Thrice Great Hermes (number three, six, and so on, and their roots), *Hermes Trismegistus*.

The Cathars saw the world as the creation of the dark force, entrapping the light within the human. But for the Church Christ was "Lord of the World" and was attributed with the role of *reconciling antagonistic elements* within creation as part of a Trinity (fig. 8.11). This acceptance of God's will within creation was at odds with the Cathar's belief in the individual soul made of just the light.

The idea of the Lord of the World implied a job to be done within it. Although it became a central tenet of Christianity, it was still an Indo-European project about the solar hero god who sacrifices himself, exem-

Figure 8.11. Jesus as Lord of the World on the central west portal of Chartres, with the four apocalyptic beasts, characterizations of the quarter days between solstice and equinoctial points. He is immediately framed by the Vesica Pisces as Lord of the Age of Pisces, the grand reconciliation of opposites, and creator of sacred spaces via √3. Other portals show the seven traditional arts/planets and the zodiac.

plified by Indra as he is described in the Vedas: "With the sun's help he made pathways throughout the darkness that extended pathless" (Rig Veda VI.21.3) implies a zodiac and "Thou becomest great by virtue of the sacred word" (Rig Veda X.50.4) implies the Logos.

> Indra is not the mere storm god which later Indian lore made him into, but his association with the sun and the finding of light (RV III.39.7a) and certain of his feats point to his fundamental psychological importance. He is the space-maker, an expression of multi-leveled meaning. He is the light-bringer whose action of severing darkness, of slaying Vritra, dragon of chaos, makes him the personification of mind's struggle for freedom.[1]

What was explicitly Indo-European was made implicitly so in western Christianity, in the doctrinal atmosphere of the Middle Ages. Perhaps this is why there were so many rumors of secret groups, groups that understood this.

THE MEDIEVAL ARTHUR MYTH AND THE CATHARS

As mentioned before, the Arthur story had moved south from Scotland to Wales as the p-Celt world of the Brythonic (indigenous) British was defeated. But Britain was already an Indo-European land, druidic Celtism being the last historical gasp of large scale ancient religious establishments. The Romans brought other influences such as the Sarmatians and the Mithraic practices of the Roman legions.

The chivalry that emerges in the medieval Arthur stories and the extreme virtue of the Cathar "perfects" (who generally exceeded Catholic monks in their austerities) was impossible to defend against the pragmatism of brutish knights eager to take up the sword and doctrinaire clerics encouraging them to take the property and lives of others. Were chivalry and heresy the moral high ground of this age? Perhaps the brutal suppression of the Cathars in the thirteenth century is understandable in the light of the threat they presented religiously and politically, with their strategic location between Aquitaine, Moorish Spain, Rome, and the kingdom of the Franks.

The newer Arthurian myths were promoted by the Plantagenet kings of England, Normans who were Dukes of Anjou. When Henry II married Eleanor of Aquitaine, the richest woman in the world, the diminutive Franc kingdom and the struggling Roman Church were facing powerful challenges. Allegiances were complex and the new Arthur material—the *Matter of Britain*—portrayed the situation by reworking and developing the mythic elements.

Chretien de Troyes wrote some of this for the court of Troy, the capital of Champagne, the principality of Hugh of Champagne, founder of the Knights Templar only a century earlier. These medieval stories had a Celtic pedigree however, such as translating Tristan and Isolde into Lancelot (from Brittany) and Guinevere, Arthur's Queen.

If we project the lunation triangle from Edinburgh onto a recent map of the Angevin Empire (fig. 8.12), Eleanor's famous chivalrous court at Poitiers and Toulouse, the capital of Catharism (and before that of the Visigoths), lie on the intermediate hypotenuse, which then runs on to Mallorca. This line is associated with the sacred marriage and perpetual choirs—how fitting it is that the troubadours come from this axis. This line should perhaps rather be called the Grail Line, especially considering that the myth of Mary Magdalene as wife of Jesus now joins Arthur and Guinevere and Tristan and Isolde as myths about the sacred marriage of male and female, Sun and Moon.

The Norman conquests were in fact continuing on as the Angevin Empire, only to be pushed back by their allies in the crusades, the northern French and the Roman Church. The politics of power blocks might have lain behind the mythmaking. The Grail emerged as a most evocative new symbol, connecting a Celtic healing bowl with a cup for the Last Supper of Christ's self-declared blood, and a sick and wasted land with knight's quest to find the Grail so as to redeem the land.

The medieval Church knew that, in this story of Arthur, it was being presented with:

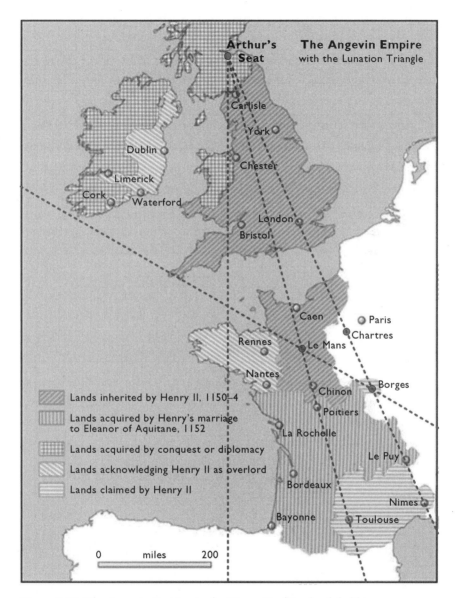

Figure 8.12. The Angevin Empire, under Henry II of England, held power over most of Britain and western France, probably taking the Matter of Britain and Arthur beyond p-Celt Brittany and into Cathar country.

1. an alternative source of myth and symbolism over which it had no direct control, and

2. a subtle heresy that, wrapped up as it was with nobility itself, would be hard to attack while maintaining the divine right of kings and other such glue which held the alliance of secular and religious authority together within the feudal system.

The Knights Templar were very close to this prototype. They were billed as noble knights on, it seems likely now, a secret quest. They had proximity to the heretical south, as their logistic support operation developed between La Rochelle on the Atlantic and Marseilles in southern France.

The many crags in the Languedoc with fairytale castles and minor feudal lords could have inspired the idea of the Grail Castle, even though the conventional interpretation places the Arthurian events in Britain (fig. 8.13). This could represent a displacement similar to that proposed

Figure 8.13. The Castle of Puilaurens blends with rock and mist, demonstrating the evocative character of castles perched on fastnesses in the Languedoc.

by Vinci of Homer's tales to the Baltic. Cathar country could have been injected to extend the myth and reflect the inner history and sources of the medieval in southern France.

In fact, the Arthur tales from the medieval period are most plausible in the mystical landscape of the French Pyrenees, the original Provence that stretched from Aquitaine to the Rhone, a culture that was virtually wiped out by the Cathar Crusades. The new tales can be seen as a reworking of Arthur and Celtic myth, with the inclusion of new influences such as chivalry, courtly love, and the mystic quest. What emerges is more zeitgeist than conspiracy, with Islamic, Cathar, and Christian influences coalescing and cross-fertilizing. The mystery of the Templars and of the Grail represent the same crossover; the first as a mysterious but real order of knights, and the other as a symbol of the Pole and its hidden redemptive and sacralizing power.

Only the provable heresy could be removed, giving birth to the first of many Inquisitions, which allowed the Franks to take the Cathar lands in the name of a crusade, and to break the Norman hold on southern and western France by the time of King John, the mythic enemy of Robin Hood and usurper of the last real Angevin hope, Richard the Lionheart.

NINE

LIFE, THE UNIVERSE, AND EVERYTHING

How did *history,* based upon invention and writing, emerge from a *prehistory* based upon measuring and monumentalizing the cosmos? In myth such a cycle could be explained as being due to the variability of precessional world ages, ages that have come into popular idiom as golden, silver, copper, and iron, as if the metals somehow represent the moral values of the ages.

In approaching this mystery, questions begging to be answered include:

1. What is different in the monotheistic view of God, so influential in the historical period?
2. Why is it impossible for modern science to find any causal explanation for the Earth mysteries?
3. How can the physical features of our planet display a level of alignment in natural features (such as the Michael Lines) and why did ancient humans build monumental structures displaying similar alignments (that is, landscape geometries)?
4. Why was the twelve-fold system associated with Jupiter-Zeus when it appears to be the solar deity that arises in the Bronze Age?

HISTORY
AND THE IDEA OF GOD

There is a strong implication in the mystical beliefs of the past that the inner life of humanity is somehow tied to the changes in the outer world—"As above, so below, as below so above." The logic behind this is two-fold. First, the universe itself represents the "exhaustion of God," in that all the potentials held in the mind of God, the numerical possibilities created with the universe, have somehow created the present world. This provides an explanation as to why God, in his active nature, cannot be known except through the universe and by us. The proof of God's existence is then dependent on whether we think the world was created by such a being or not. This optional nature of belief in God is actually a powerful virtue because it means that, as thinking beings within the creation, humans do not live in God's pocket—should God exist. This gives us the power to be an active force, to do both good and bad things, and to be exactly "as gods."

Secondly, therefore, the creation of our own lives and the building of civilizations of different types represent the ways in which the human potential actually becomes applied within this world. The creation of a new civilization takes place at its inception when relatively small forces define the roots that will set the tone for all that follows. Therefore humanity can follow the story of creation in that the ideas of a civilization also become exhausted through exploring *the potential of the ideas* present at that civilization's inception.

In this way, the megalithic culture can be seen as being based upon the study of the objective world, itself based upon a numerical model of that world's creation. From this an idea of God, a creator, would have naturally emerged. It is my proposal that this *Idea of God* came to replace the *Works of God* at the inception of the historical period.

The Idea of God, in the singular, is different from God. The Works of God are different than the things people do because of the Idea of God. The basic components of these two statements can be shown in a table as:

"PREHISTORIC"	"HISTORIC"
God	The Idea of God
Works of God	Works of the Idea of God

The right hand side of this table is the reflection of the left in the human mind; the above has a noumenal quality, while the below has a phenomenal character. We can only see the Works of God and not God, and the Idea of God is really *only surmised* through works that describe God.

This distinction is necessary if there is to be any hope of seeing the differences within the overall field of human thought about God. Obviously religions exist in the human mind as the Idea of God, and yet they are always striving, or even pretending, to have fused the Idea of God with God. How this is achieved is interesting.

An example of attempted fusion is the Word or Logos. As scripture, texts like the Bible come to be claimed as being the Work of God, while evidently they come about as just being works based on the Idea of God. There is even sufficient confusion here to allow scripture to *become* the Word of God or Logos, in which the structure of the information *is a creation*. Then, using the idea of immanence, as with Jesus as Son of God, the works become God on Earth as revealed scripture.

The Idea of God can be an evolved and valid mechanism for knowing God, because the Works of God are the only way a *transcendent* God could be known. Thus, for instance, when a physicist demonstrates that nuclear fusion can explain stars, the tuning of cosmic constants allowing this to be the case can, in the anthropic theories, be inferred to be a Work of God. This can lead to an Idea of God. Indeed, it is entirely likely that ancient cultures such as the megalithic could have inferred that the movement of the celestial bodies was a Work of God, so that their Idea of God could have proceeded from this type of working, which perhaps needs a name such as God as Maker, or in Greek, *demiurge*. This type of functioning links the Works and Idea of God.

But was the megalithic culture a religion? In the sense of "reconnecting to the Whole," then the word *religion* appears to have been coined exactly to describe the type of religion that existed in the ancient world, the world of prehistory, because there was a direct link between factual measurement and divine speculation.

This direct link is not found in modern religions and therefore we must now ask: What do the moderns have and how does this relate to the evolution of ideas through prehistory into history? History can be seen in terms of religion up until the point where the Idea of God became a choice. In other words prior religious thought was mainly compulsive, though not always oppressive. Further, the Idea of God became a political statement that God was superior but similar to leaders and priests. The idea of king and then the idea of church were presented as the Works of God, when these were in fact Works of the Idea of God.

If there is to be any continuity between prehistory and history, in the evolution of the Idea of God, it has to be that *as a meme** the Idea of God—a symbol—*became* God: the God of historic religion became a false God, simply by the definition that no idea can pretend to be the thing it purports to describe without being false, that is, a substitute for the very thing that gives it any meaning in the first place. This kind of religion claims the world is created by God, but says that the Works of God are not to be studied but rather treated as a stage set for the drama of human belief in the Idea of God.

Some catastrophe must have occurred, at least in the inner life of humanity, as the historic period dawned, which cut the Idea of God loose from its moorings of being based upon the Works of God. The preexisting material about God and gods, evolved from the late Neolithic period, was turned into various pieces of sacred literature that told humankind what God wanted humanity to think and do. The Works of God changed from being the universe to being the Word; those that followed the Word became the people of God and the others sinners, in that their works were not the Works of God.

The creation of such religions became the rule within the historic

---

*"The term *meme* (from the Greek word *mimema* for 'something imitated') first came into popular use with the publication of the book *The Selfish Gene* by Richard Dawkins in 1976. Dawkins defined the meme as 'a unit of cultural transmission, or a unit of imitation'." (Wikipedia)

period. Such religions live within wholly defined limits, so that the evo-lution of thought is controlled. Any important set of ideas has to have a set of corresponding symbols or jargon within the system; thus the gods were transliterated into saints, calendars were derived from festivals on saints' days, and so on. In fact, only the sacred calendar remains as a direct connection to the Works of God, such as is the case with the lunar month, solar year, Venus synod, and so on.

The mental landscapes of religious thought often allow for mysti-cal wings, brotherhoods and so on, which function like a subconscious for the religious culture. They must always remain hidden or occult if there is not to be an authority crisis and subsequent crackdown, as may have occurred with the Knights Templar. The old Atlantis-style informa-tion appears to have survived through such secret groups. Thus "pri-vate clubs" of the Works of God, such as the Benedictine and Cistercian orders, used ancient knowledge of Earth and its energies in the service of their Church.

The alarming picture that emerges of the historical period is that those responsible for leading historical cultures appear to know things that are forbidden within the mindset of the culture itself. The things they know belong to the genuine nature of the Works of God, and an elite develops the science of manipulating the Idea of God to control the culture. Such groups might speak of the Great Work, which cannot be known by the non-elites and which justifies any means to achieve their perceived Works of God. In other words, the equation of the Works of the Idea of God with the Works of God operates in service to their myth.

The time of the megalithic and other truly prehistoric-style cultures can be viewed as an age in which the Works of God were studied within the observable world processes. This led to Ideas of God, probably based upon number, and a sophisticated language of symbols and correspon-dences within the observable world. These two things became detached when the Idea of God started to be informed directly by means of philo-sophical speculation, famously by the classical Greek schools.

The process of abstract thought is based upon symbols and equa-tions between different symbols. We know that there must be some kind of functionality such as memes operating in the human brain, whereby ideas can influence behavior, especially cognitive behavior. It is entirely true that systems of thought are a form of group mind, and that evolution has obviously not ceased in the human but has moved to a different area of mental operations, which can affect survival. Our cultural norms about personal freedom actually work to prevent us from experiencing whatever would happen if we thought we were not free, but in fact owned by a greater distributed being called our culture, a culture that can only change according to definite laws.

Do the Works of God include what is happening to us, and what happened in prehistoric times? It seems entirely likely, but to understand why obliges us to study, in prehistoric style, the Works of God! The break with tradition that was coterminous with the onset of history—written language, abstract thought, and technical innovation—was an "accident waiting to happen," related to the development of notation as a power tool for studying the Works of God. When the brain enters the symbolic work of a notational system, it has broken off the thing from the thing notated. Then the symbol can have a life independent from the phenomena it represents: An eclipse can be calculated without the eclipse moment, the full moon predicted years before the event.

THE GHOST IN THE MACHINE

Now we consider why it is impossible for modern science to find any causal explanation for the Earth mysteries. The general area of Earth mysteries could be understood by adapting some of the ideas John Bennett had about the role of determining or "framework" conditions, which are the conditions for anything to exist at all, which lie behind any possible phenomenon. In brief these emerge from the idea that the universe, at each highly structured point, combines the characteristics of space with those of potential structures and reentrant processes. These Bennett called "space, eternity, and hyparxis." Eternity relates to timeless pattern and directions in space while hyparxis relates to recurrence in time and rotation in space. Framework conditions exist on many scales and some are specialized according to location, as seen with planetary orbits and rotation. Any three elements can combine to form six different orderings, or triads. The systematic view of this is the hexad, which has the systemic attribute of coalescence, meaning "to come together in one body or mass."[1]

We are here concerned with the spirit of a given place or the characteristics of the planet as a manifestation of its framework conditions. There can be no doubt that Earth is subject to a powerful and highly specific framework such as the numerical environment found within planetary orbits and its axial spin.

> We should therefore fix our attention on the third spatial direction [related to Hyparxis], that in simple situations is associated with spin and the axis of angular momentum [e.g. of Earth], but on the macroscopic scale is associated with the properties of *form, scale* and *proportion.*[2]

These all appear to have no *causal* relationship to conditions on Earth beyond the variations in heating of the surface and some tidal effects upon all water to which cellular life is sensitive. This lack of causation is symptomatic of the way framework operates outside of time: Its effects arise out of the configuration of the universe, whereas causation is predicated as a sequence of cause leading to effects, or one thing acting on another thing.

This alone is a valuable insight into why these Earth mysteries, in which a kind of power is attributed to the land itself, are mysterious. In the context of the Western historical process, now endemic, there is a strong component of causality and actualization. In prehistory, on the other hand, there is strong evidence of oracles and geomantic activity, which may have been based upon *receptivity to framework conditions,* a kind of not-doing. A whole area of phenomena is completely filtered out of modern awareness because of our focus on cause and effect, especially when targeting control over our environment, personal gain, and security. The prehistoric approach may have been similar to the Spirit culture centered in China, which has a surviving tradition of geomancy called feng shui, and Taoist, Buddhist, Chan, and Zen schools that focus on a timeless framework, almost at the expense of actualization.

The way Bennett's framework laws operate is *out of time;* hence he called them the Laws of Synchronicity. Psychologist C. G. Jung—with the physicist Wolfgang Pauli—also studied synchronicity, which means "disparate things coming together in a meaningful way that has no causal explanation." Another word for synchronicity is *co-incidence.* For example when there is a co-incidence of crags along a straight line, a geologist who cannot provide a rational causal explanation for its existence will simply dismiss it as a coincidence. Similarly, a numerical set of planetary cycles (as found in my book *Matrix of Creation*) or the Saturn calendar (discussed in chapter 1) do not make much impression on an astronomer because causal astronomy is inimical to ideas such as the music of the spheres, Bode's law, astrology, and Platonic geometry, all of which fly in the face of causal rationality. Similarly, a historian would hardly like the idea that the places where Normans lived informed their historical performance.

If, for one moment, acausal events are entertained as being possible, along with the possibility that they may be structured by the general state of the universe and local configurations of land, then we stand in front of a mystery largely ignored for at least 2000 years, though it has survived in such "superstitions" as astrology or divination, and has even become quite fashionable as in the case of feng shui. Most of our theories of the unknown tend to take the form of interaction with beings from other stars or dimensions, or after or before death, or as angels; most of them are based upon our fear of the unknown. We have populated the unknown with beings, God being a perfect example. The idea that the universe has immediate consequences of its own dimensionality, not as a being but through the immediate consequence of its structure, has fallen away largely through the pride of the human maker of tools, the *do-er.*

The framework worldview is more natural to women since the paradigm is very akin to the universe giving birth to the spirit of place, the universe being the Creatrix of what we call Earth mysteries. The transfer from matriarchy to patriarchy is another congruent feature of the move from prehistory to history.

TOWARD AN ETHEREAL EARTH

Physical features of the planet sometimes seem to display a level of alignment between natural features, but the geological explanation of the Michael Lines or any other leylines within the landscape (stretching over continents, in great circles or rhumb lines of constant bearing) will never work as a primary mechanism. Yet if such alignments are brought about by *acausal* framework conditions, then any clues will seem unlikely and will be difficult to see, especially when filtered through the methodology of modern science.

Solar eclipses can, once every few thousand years, trace out almost exactly the path of these lines, at these latitudes, depending upon the relative placement of the lunar node. The Moon passes the Sun and its shadow is always going west. At a descending node, where the Moon is going below the Sun, the shadow can pass St. Michael's Mount and travel to Mount Carmel as in figure 9.1. A similar picture exists for the Michael Line of England into the Baltic. There are people that believe eclipses have an effect, representing as they do the eclipse of the solar. But this effect deeply involves our own consciousness, which can never be separated from it.

A better framework in which to look for an answer appears to be the ethereal world of projective geometry, as pursued in the *Anthroposophy* of Rudolf Steiner. Also called non-Euclidean geometry, it incorporates the idea of the infinite and turns conventional ideas of geometry on their head. Circles and ellipses can be formed through very simple generative rules involving straight lines. Spheres and the elliptically deformed sphere of Earth can be generated using two invariant planes touching the North and South Poles (fig. 9.2). In projective geometry we start from the whole and generate the parts, or start from infinity and produce the finite. What is done in this mathematics is to replicate the influence of *form* on phenomena.

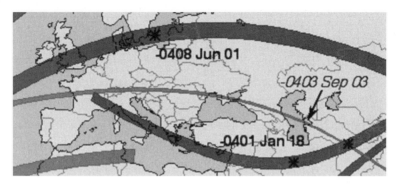

Figure 9.1. A total eclipse traveled down the Apollo Line in 401 B.C.E. (Illustration courtesy of Fred Espenak, NASA/GSFC.)

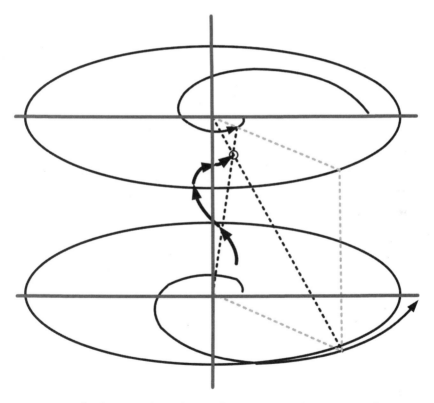

Figure 9.2. The drawing of a path curve between two polar invariant planes. The inner twisting and arrowed line is a result of the intersection of two dotted lines, one end of each of which follows one of the polar spirals while the other end is fixed to the opposite pole.

To generate the shape of Earth from without involves equiangular spirals growing out of each of these polar planes. Every point upon the resulting Earth-like shape is then defined by the crossing of lines from the northern and southern spiral plane. There are then certain *path curves* that run over this surface at definite angles. Such path curves can be seen clearly in the patterns of seeds in a pine cone and many other natural "packing solutions" (fig. 9.3).

It is interesting that many ancient sites have carved spirals while spirals are rarely seen in nature *except* for those found as a result of path curve generating processes. The idea is that a higher cause is present, from a world of pure pattern, using geometry to define something that informs, to a degree, the material alignments over time upon Earth. Lucien Richer tells us that the Apollo Line is a *rhumb line,* a line of constant bearing, which is a spherical spiral rather than a great circle around Earth. According to Wikipedia a spherical spiral (rhumb line) is:

Figure 9.3. The number of clockwise and counterclockwise spirals in a sunflower are always two consecutive Fibonacci numbers.

. . . the curve on a sphere traced by a ship traveling from one pole to the other while keeping a fixed angle (but not a right angle) with respect to the meridians of longitude, i.e. keeping the same bearing. The curve has an infinite number of revolutions, with the distance between them decreasing as the curve approaches either of the poles.

The pine cones and seed heads displaying such path curves generally appear in books on sacred geometry as examples of the Golden Mean or of the related Fibonacci series. It is central to Steiner's vision that such geometries lie at the core of an etheric world and that this etheric is really the framework of the universe out to infinity, that is, it derives exactly from what Bennett has described as framework conditions.

If Earth's "etheric body" is defined from the poles, then Bennett's advice is to "fix our attention on the third spatial direction associated with spin and the axis of angular momentum." This concurs with the ancient importance given to the Pole as a source of the framework, the creator of which has withdrawn and is somehow distant. In ancient divination, a critical role is given to a central empty point of the intersection of two orders, such as that of "Heaven" and "Earth." Following the simple manual instructions for drawing an elliptical sphere displays path curves that follow an angle of about 30° to north–south as in figure 9.4.

The invariant planes touch the North and South Poles and would have spiral growth patterns, reduced here to sample points connected to the opposite pole. The intersections of the northern and southern lines define the shape of Earth as an oblate spheroid with path curves that would be equiangular rhumb lines at 30° to north–south.

This is a far more satisfactory hypothesis than attributing a causal connection to eclipse paths. It is in harmony with traditional ideas and provides a subsisting framework for the pattern of places upon Earth as an objective, *though acausal,* structure. Just as the medieval cathedral imposed a specific ratio into the creation of its internal space, the geometry shown describes Earth formally rather than materially via path curves describing the surface.

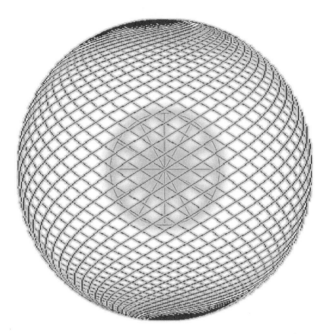

Figure 9.4. Path curves that would behave like the Michael Line upon an Earth created by projective geometry as its formal cause.

For the path curves to be coherent in the landscape the whole framework would have to be rotating with the crust, including the north and south spiral planes. They cross each other in families forming a hexagon at a given parallel of latitude. Such a hexagon can be seen like a cap upon the pole of Saturn.

While the techniques of projective geometry are in the public domain through the Steiner publishing houses, little detailed research is easily available, apart from *The Vortex of Life* by Laurence Edwards. In his life's work, Edwards primarily studied the bud shapes of a variety of plant species photographically. This allowed him to develop what was then a state-of-the-art photo analysis tool to derive the very few parameters that completely describe a given complex path curve, especially its lambda, which is—in the case of the spheroid between two planar spirals as in figure 9.5—the ratio of growth in the two spirals. Where the lambda is not one, the shape produced is like a pine cone and somewhat "pear-shaped."

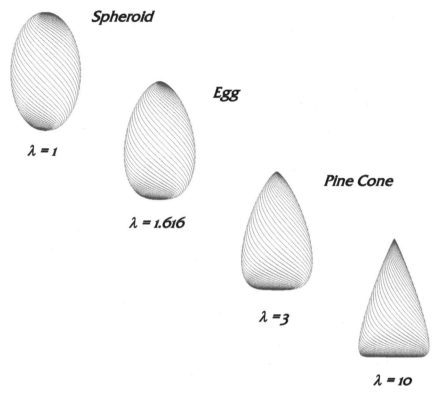

Figure 9.5. The path curves generated by projective geometry are a range of egg shapes in cross section. They can be as simple as an ellipse or even a circle when the growth rate of the polar spirals is equal. It is this condition that allows a shape like Earth to be generated from this technique. (Adapted from Nick Thomas, see his website, www.nct.anth.org.uk.)

Edwards found that the lambda varied in a scientifically significant way with the lunar month, relative to one or other of the planets. Thus some species would have a response to the Moon and Saturn, others the Moon and Jupiter, and so on. Normally, we think of the lunar month or the lunar orbit. The first is its period relative to the Sun, while the second, the period relative to the stars, is considered fixed. What is little known is that, because Saturn and Jupiter slowly move, the Moon takes longer than a single orbit to repeat the same aspect to them also—creating a new species of month, quite invisible and just longer than the lunar orbit.

The Saturn–Moon (P_{S-M}) synod is 27.391 days and the Jupiter–Moon (P_{J-M}) synod is 27.495 days. From this:

1. The synodic period of Saturn (378.09 days) includes 13.80 Saturn–Moon synods and 12.80 lunar months:
   a. 12.80 ÷ 0.80 = 16, showing how the Saturn relationship to the Moon marks out the 15:16 relationship of the Saturn synod to the lunar year, found in the Saturn calendar (see chapter 1).
   b. The unit difference between 12.80 and 13.80 shows that Sun, Moon, and Saturn are locked in resonance to produce this 15:16 half tone.
2. Similarly, the synodic period of Jupiter (398.88 days) includes 14.50 Jupiter–Moon synods and 13.50 lunar months:
   a. 13.50 ÷ 1.5 = 9, showing how the Jupiter relationship to the Moon marks out the 8:9 relationship of the Jupiter synod to the lunar year (found in chapter 9 of my book *Matrix of Creation*).
   b. The unit difference between 13.50 and 14.50 shows that Sun, Moon, and Jupiter are locked in resonance to produce this 8:9 whole tone.

The perfect tones present in these rhythms are apparently picked up by plants, whose form alters according to the point within these cycles that growth proceeds. The point here is that nature appears to operate using path curves. We can best understand this in the context of a system of extraordinary value developed by Aristotle, probably the most approved-of philosopher of the medieval Church. In order to approach what things were made of, he composed a scheme involving four terms: formal cause, material cause, efficient cause, and final cause (fig. 9.6).

Aristotle reached, by stages, the conclusion that the arising of any significant object requires the combination of four independent terms. He began with the dyad of matter and form . . . we have a

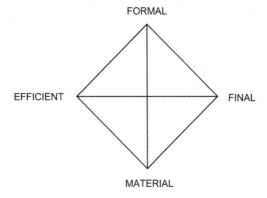

Figure 9.6. Aristotle's Four Causes or Sources.

wooden bed and a marble statue. Wood and marble are the matter; bed and statue are the form. He goes on to say that wood does not become a bed by itself, so there must be a third factor that causes it to change. Mere change, however, is not enough; it [the matter] must be directed and guided toward the forms. There are thus two operative factors, one the efficient cause that produces the change, and the other the final cause that directs it toward its end which is the form.[3]

The efficient cause is most clearly seen in the tools and techniques of the craftsman, while inspiration, experience, and sensitivity best express the achievement of the final form. In the context of a planet, the crust is evidently the material cause. The processes of geology including subduction, convection, metamorphosis, and tectonic plates are efficient causes, as are climate and the dynamical effects of wind and waves.

The formal cause or "informing structure" of Earth can be derived from a path curve, which can *naturally develop ellipses,* unlike abstract crystal prototypes or Platonic solids. The shaping of Earth is not then a plan built from the material world and formulated by a being, but is instead a simple top-down concept arising out of spinning something. Science does not *need* to say this is true or false.

The derivation of the shape can be by deformation due to spin as an *efficient cause* while at the same time obeying the derivation, as all such shapes do, of projective geometry as its *formal cause*. Edwards gathered his data over many years up until his death but it will be awhile before the impact of this eminent effort will be appreciated more generally.*

A *final cause* might predicate some type of sensitivity within the crust, which is of course dramatically shown by the role of life in shaping the geosphere, let alone its influence on the oceans and atmosphere. It has been noted by Vernadski, father of biogeochemistry, that biological processes play a large part in the actualization of the crust, even discounting recent human influences.† Minerals carried in the bodies, living or dead, of plants and animals contribute significantly to the variety of rock and quality of soils available in current landscapes, and the regulation of climate through the carbon cycle. Other factors are the vertical convection and horizontal coriolis cells, coriolis forces being caused by spin. Any free bodies moving within a rotational framework, as on the surface of the spinning Earth, are deflected continuously away from forward motion, leading to the spirals we see as weather systems.

If path curve geometry is the *formal cause* of Earth's surface, then its numerical roots are remarkably simple and have the ability to describe lines upon the surface exactly because, in truth, the continuous surface of such a shape is only a composite of such paths, unlike the material view that they are made up of a planar surface, the entity we call the crust.

THE MARK OF ZEUS

The last of the questions posed at the beginning of this chapter concerns the relationship of the twelve-fold system to the king of the gods,

---

*The fear of bolstering the astrological hypothesis naturally holds back scientific scrutiny of such work.

†Vernadski expressed a fundamental law of the biosphere as tending toward the maximum amount and speed of transport of materials over Earth's surface. This is an expression of a final cause. The formal cause stemming from the nature of the planet itself informs this tendency, so it has both causal and teleological sides.

Jupiter-Zeus. In my book *Matrix of Creation*, I showed many numerical relationships of Jupiter to Earth time including an approximate
eleven to twelve relationship of solar year to Jupiter synod, this in bal-
ance with the same ratio between lunar and solar year. The lunar year
has twelve months within the solar year, whereas the zodiac divides up
the solar year *exactly* as a complete round of the Sun—by definition.

So what divides the ecliptic into twelve? The simplest answer
appears in the oldest bona-fide Indo-European system of all, that of the
Indian astronomers. Conventionally they are thought to have received
the zodiac of twelve signs from the Greeks. However, they have a unique
type of year within what they call the Jupiter Cycle or *Brihaspati Sam-
vatsara* that lasts about sixty years.

This Jupiter Cycle is well known to Western astronomers and led
to the phenomenon of the Trigon, which records the successive conjunctions of Jupiter and the slower-moving Saturn (see fig. 9.7). It is an
example of a time period that exceeds the individual period of any single
body, being a *grand conjunction* of the two outermost visible planets. It
has been proposed that this period could have been used to calibrate the
precessional ages* and also that it might have been part of the "passing of the measure" from Saturn to Jupiter, these bodies also having a
Golden Mean relationship (see fig. 9.8).

Sixty was traditionally associated with Jupiter but there are not a
full sixty solar years in this cycle. Instead, the period in question, called
Barhaspatya samvantara (literally, "disciple of Brihaspati period") is
the time taken for Jupiter to pass through one sign of the twelve-fold
zodiac. This is 361 days, numerically nineteen squared.† With regard to

---

*The usual, canonical length is 25,920 which, divided by twelve, is 2,160 years per pre-
cessional age. Dividing this by a perfect sixty yields a perfect thirty-six Trigon periods.
Reversing the process based on an actual Trigon of 59.334 years gives an age of 2,136
years and a precessional cycle of 25,632 years, which is close to a typical scientific estimate of around 25,725 years.

†The manifold of time relating to nineteen is deserving of its own book since the Moon
in Saros and Metonic periods completes periods involving nineteen eclipse or solar years
echoing Jupiter's own involvement with this number. Robin Heath's books cover many
parts of this "nineteen complex" of celestial phenomena.

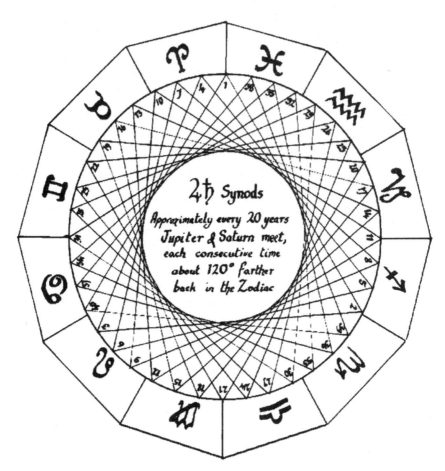

Figure 9.7. The Trigon Jupiter-Saturn cycle. About every twenty years Jupiter conjuncts Saturn again, and in three conjunctions this happens close to the stars of the first conjunction, to form a triangle. (Drawing by Robin Heath.)

the zodiac, it does not matter whether it came from the Greeks, or if the Indians already had it, or both had obtained it or who invented it. There is an objective fact here, that the zodiac of twelve *is seen as defined* by the Trigon period, that is, by the combined behavior of Jupiter and Saturn, the latter being the reputed "previous" ruler to the former.

Therefore—although it looks like the Indians have based their Jupiter passing through a zodiacal sign of a pre-existing zodiac—it is actually *Jupiter that defines the zodiac* as 1/60 of its movement within a whole Trigon period. Interestingly, therefore, the sexidecimal system of

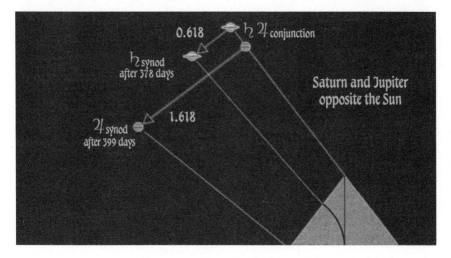

Figure 9.8. Golden Mean relationship between Jupiter and Saturn.

the Babylonians is perfectly set up for counting this cycle and appears to form the prototype or authority for this system.* Also worthy of note is the deeply canonical nature of the number sixty (formula $2^2 \times 3 \times 5$) which displays all the characteristics of harmony since it only contains the harmonic primes.

We have seen that Saturn is characteristic of the number seven, with time periods in days naturally being divisible by the week, Saturn to Jupiter synods being in the ratio of 18:19 three week periods of twenty-one days. The excess of the Saturn synod over the solar year can be divided by the excess of the Jupiter synod over that of Saturn to yield the Golden Mean ratio. In the Trigon therefore, each one third of which takes twenty *Barhaspatya samvantaras* of 361 days for Jupiter to traverse twenty signs of the zodiac, each "year" has a different sign of the zodiac exactly like the Chinese system of twelve animals associated with solar years† (remembering that the zodiac is a "belt of animals").

This fact gives Jupiter a role in creating the star signs while making

---

*Note also we have yet another year, forming the series 360, 361, 364, 365, 365.242 days.

†These are Horse, Goat-Ram-Sheep, Monkey, Rooster, Dog, Boar-Pig, Rat-Mouse, Ox, Tiger, Rabbit-Hare, Dragon, and Snake.

him king of the gods for the post-Saturnian pantheon. He has a whole tone relation (8:9) to the lunar year of twelve months while Saturn has the half tone of 15:16.

There is a tradition of a ruler being given a rod or measure, from which comes the ability to divide up correctly, which is connected to the theme of enchantment. While Figure 9.8 shows the Golden Mean being passed between the two planets, in this case the ratio of *Barhaspatya samvantara* (361.048 days) to the Jupiter synod (398.88 days) times three equals the astronomical megalithic yard or AMY found in megalithic Britain (99.998% accurate). Therefore, this same ratio is the foot for this archaic yard. It is the measure of Jupiter, in spite of being a polar measure (1.728 times 11/7 feet), as would normally be associated with the Pole and *Saturnian* priestly power.

The other astronomical derivation of the AMY is the lunar month divided by the excess of the solar year over the lunar year, with an even greater accuracy of 99.99996%. Thus Jupiter controls the most fundamental aspects of time on Earth, the solar and lunar years, with his measure based upon the zodiac-Trigon and his own synod.*

Jupiter's system of time is occult compared to that of Saturn, described in chapter 1 and based upon the number seven, the week of seven days. Yet it incorporates all sorts of new ideas based upon harmony and hence the first three prime numbers (two, three, and five). This undoubtedly would have led to the universe having being seen by ancient humans as an evolved creation, and they left record of their understanding within their calendars, monuments, myths, and landscape geometries, as presented within this book.

---

*That said though, systems should be considered as a whole since they depend upon all their parts to function.

TEN

BUILDING THE NEW JERUSALEM

Sufficient evidence exists that a large input of sacred geometry and hence Atlantean number lore entered the Gothic civilization of the Middle Ages. This evidence is strongly associated with the Normans and Burgundians in particular. They played a crucial role, first in making contact with the Muslim world before and after the First Crusade, and then in the creation of the Knights Templar and Cistercian religious orders that were quasi-independent from the Church and super successful in their expansion throughout Christendom and beyond.

While the Islamic world of this era was laden with knowledge that had disappeared during the West's Dark Ages following the fall of the Roman Empire, this knowledge appears to have resurfaced together with some indigenous knowledge and quite probably some Jewish material discovered by the Knights Templar beneath the Temple Mount. These three sources created a new synthesis of knowledge that had originally been prehistoric in character, knowledge based upon a worldview that number was in some way sacred because the creation of the world displayed numerical rules that could be simply read through informed observation.

The new religious orders that embraced this "new" knowledge operated only in accordance with its dictates because it was *ipso facto* heretical and placed the knower above the law of the Church. Being privy to genuine historical information revealed to these orders the limitations of the Church's fixed creed and version of history. In any case, the ruling class of nobles was already a race apart from their feudal tenants, and the clerics, often noble themselves, were placed in charge of the canon law that set the limits of aristocratic behavior. As a result it was not unusual during this time for kings and nobles to go through periods of excommunication as a normal negotiating posture or simply to delay resolution while gaining advantages.

At the height of the Angevin empire, the Knights Templar appear to have been engaged in the task of working out how to integrate their new knowledge within the culture, while preserving its major themes. This explains most simply why secret building techniques were employed, such as those found at Chartres after 1200 C.E. These monuments were public works holding both geomantic relevance and cultural power. The Templars' second task was to hide the sources of this knowledge and their power in safe places and build an infrastructure capable of taking the organization into the future, beyond the crusading period.

The Templars' *stated* duty was to protect pilgrims, and for this they needed castles, ships and other logistical resources, and a multi-national organization. Gifts of land and income from land and noble sons, combined with crusading fever in the donor nations of northern Europe, built up a wealth of Templar and Cistercian establishments alike.

LAYING OUT THE BORNHOLM PATTERN

The logistical base of the Templars enabled them to conduct secret activities beyond the scrutiny of the Church. Before the death of Bernard of Clairvaux, a project was being conceived with the king and archbishop of Denmark to bring Christianity to the Baltic.[1] That the Baltic was a sacred landscape in megalithic times is shown by the many monuments there; specifically, the island of Bornholm must have been a holy island, judging by the thousands of miniature golden offerings found on the island. Thus this project represented a full turning of the wheel: from a prehistory in which the Indo-Europeans descended to Greece to turn the

Sun god into the Son of God, to the enactment, along the Apollo and Michael Lines, of historical events such as the Crusades, which defined the coming of the Western world. This would bring the prehistoric "men from the north" and all that they had found in the south back to one of their Bronze Age hunting grounds, making a complete cycle of Indo-European migration to the south and back.

The complexities of establishing a further crusade in the Baltic included bypassing the dominance of the Holy Roman Emperor in Germany and of having a favorable pope in office. After Bernard's death the conditions were right for Denmark to front a crusade against the pagan Wends who were blocking trade in the Russian rivers from the Mediterranean and abducting Christians from the Wend homelands on the southern coast of the Baltic Sea and selling them into a flourishing slave trade.

Once Templar logistics were applied to the Baltic, a special type of fortified church was developed for Baltic islands and mainland alike. Based upon their experiences of operating against the Muslims, these designs were often round in shape and more like castles, examples of which may be found on the islands of Bornholm, Oland, and Gotland.

Oland and Gotland are both on the Baltic extension of the Michael Line (fig. 10.1). Bornholm is the strategic gateway into the Baltic and was subject to considerable building of fortified churches that conformed to a mysterious sacred geometry as well as, in some cases, having portals aligned

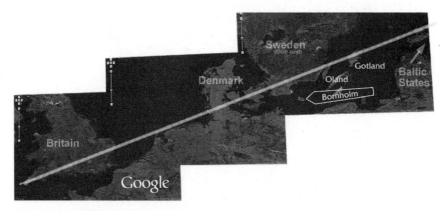

Figure 10.1. The Baltic Michael Line and relevance of islands to the Baltic Crusade when using sea power.

to the solsticial Sun. As usual, there is no clear evidence of who built this pattern of churches, and indeed the charge of seeing patterns where none exist might be made. However, Haagensen and Lincoln demonstrate that there are strong and exact coincidences present, exactly like those found within numerical creationism and within ancient landscape temples.

But insight into the pattern of Bornholm offers strong indications that the ancient methodology was secretly employed on the island. As discussed in chapter 5, the most important act in geomancy is to define a center.[2] Since Bornholm is an island, not far from the Nordic islands of Scotland, our first step is to find the longest line, on land, either north–south or on any bearing across the island (fig. 10.2).

With the center noted, the first finding of Haagensen and Lincoln[3] can be considered: Two lines drawn through the centers of Bornholm's four round churches (two churches per line) intersect at a 30° angle to each other (fig. 10.3).

The four churches appear to give a key in an ancient geomantic sense. As we have seen, the angle of 30° is part of the Michael complex of many characters, including Mercury. Similarly, many geometric figures such as the cube, vesica, hexagon, and equilateral triangle incorporate

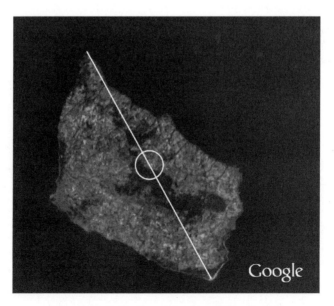

Figure 10.2. Finding the center of Bornholm.

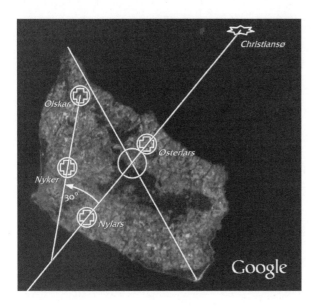

Figure 10.3. Lines connecting the round churches of Bornholm define a 30° angle and an axis that goes through the center of the island before traveling north to the islet of Christiansø. This same bearing, traveling south, is simultaneously that of Rennes-le-Château in Languedoc, southern France.

it. However, only when the preliminary work of finding the centerline for the whole island is done does it become clear that the line connecting the two churches, Osterlars and Nylars, also crosses the centerline *at its center*. It seems likely therefore that the builders, probably Templars, surveyed the island to define its center using the ancient technique then still current within the Norse tradition.

Two miraculous circumstances relate to the same bearing as the churches. The first is that the islet of Christiansø—the only other piece still above water of the ancient mountain that once made up Bornholm—is on this bearing. The second is that this same bearing defines an alignment that points to Rennes-le-Château. Further, Rennes-le-Château and Bornholm define a 30° sector relative to Jerusalem, as stated by Haagensen and Lincoln (fig. 10.4). While the distance of these two places to Jerusalem is not equal, as these authors suggest, the bearing between them does match the axis defined by the two main round churches on Bornholm. The thirty degree motif is therefore a relevant clue.

Returning to more mundane matters, such as the practical task of surveying the island, one soon notices some other strange angular relationships within the island when viewed from the southern end of the centerline (fig. 10.5).

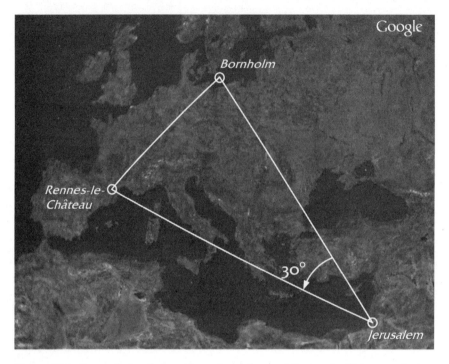

Figure 10.4. Bornholm's relationship to Jerusalem and Rennes-le-Château, echoing the 30° angle found between Bornholm's round churches and the main axis of the island. The Apollo Line travels to Britain within this "zodiacal" sector.

The chosen axis, through the two churches, strikes Bornholm from the south at 40° from the centerline when viewed from the southern tip of that centerline. Christiansø is that same angle from the centerline on the opposite side. Two faces of a nine sided figure could therefore be drawn neatly using only these three reference points. However, the chosen center for the pattern, yet to be revealed, appears to have been created by choosing Osterlars to be 10° to the right of the centerline.

Tom Graham has analyzed Bornholm from Haagensen and Lincoln's work to generate a grid over the island of sixteen by sixteen squares, each $\sqrt{3}$ of an English mile square. This is indicative of a $\sqrt{3}$ based geometry and indeed, Haagensen and Lincoln find a Star of David/hexagonal geometry in which the distance between Osterlars and Nylars is the radius of a circle, and therefore a key *measurement* for the pattern.

The distance between the two churches is known with great accu-

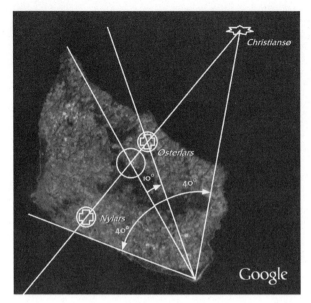

*Figure 10.5.
Establishing Osterlars
as 10° from the
centerline and finding
the limits of the chosen
axis as +/– 40° from
the bearing of the
centerline, as seen
from the southern tip
of the island.*

racy as they were used as datums for more recent surveying of the island itself. It is 14,335.585 meters, which is 8.9076 miles and thence found to be precisely √3 times 36/7 English miles.* The square root of three arises whenever a triangle is formed that has a shortest side of one unit and a hypotenuse of two units, and in this case the basic unit is 36/7 miles which is 10,000 astronomical megalithic yards (AMY).

As we have seen, this unit was last consciously used in megalithic times and forms an important part of the metrology of the lunation triangles of Britain, two such units being exactly nine royal miles long. For instance the Lundy to Stonehenge distance of 108 royal miles divides by nine to yield twelve, and nine royal miles is therefore the correct unit for that 12:13:5 Pythagorean triangle (fig. 4.18).

As figure 10.6 shows, the distances between the two churches reveals a triangular grid that is rational with respect to 10,000 AMYs that, being angled thirty degrees to the main axis, allows root three geometries to be laid out upon the land. We cannot know whether the origins of such a procedure was Nordic, Jewish, Islamic, or Atlantean, or even all of

---

*The accuracy is so high at 99.99967% as to be an exact measure in practice.

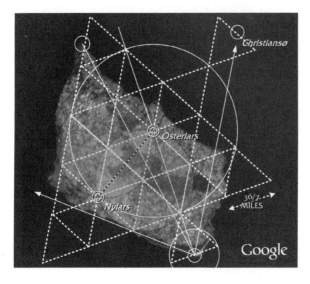

Figure 10.6. The implicit triangular grid defined by the builders of Bornholm's churches in which each dotted section is 36/7 English miles and two such are nine royal miles in length.

these, but the discovery of a megalithic unit of length and of a natural root three surveying style leads to the conclusion that a highly coherent process was being used at Bornholm, a process that was, of necessity, secret and certainly pre-Christian in origin.

Not only was a nine-fold system of forty-degree angles employed but also, apparently, a radiant of 360/36 degrees, that is, ten-degree bearings were established. This appears to be part of a surveying toolkit since, in Bornholm, the Nylars–Osterlars distance also has a Golden Mean relationship to the Nylars–Christiansø distance, as is found in each arm of a pentagon star. As with the Knave of Clubs tarot card, useful rules of thumb and possibly higher knowledge can be embedded into such grids and sightlines, which can generate sacred geometry without a difficult derivation from first principles.

INTO THE SUNSET, WITH THE ENLIGHTENMENT

The Bornholm operation represents a lesser known part of a modern myth involving Templar treasures, both gold and knowledge, that was on the move from Jerusalem and between preceptories. It is thought that, long before their suppression, one or more secret *caches* moved to southern France and one unit may have moved to Bornholm, ready for a move West, to what would eventually become the United States. The only traces we have in the realm of fact are in the practices of sacred geometry such as the secret geometry behind the construction of brand new cities such as Bath, Edinburgh, and Washington, D.C. (fig. 10.7).

It took centuries for the Church to lose its grip over the population, which it had gained at the advent of the Gothic. Forces such as plague and Mongol hordes wore the culture down, while simultaneously a brave new world of exploration was starting up. The ability to "think out of the box" and go beyond classical thought was literal when going beyond the limit of the maps of Ptolemy, where Jerusalem was marked at the center.

The Templars were routed by the king of France in 1307. He was heavily in debt to them and their power and wealth had by then no obvious purpose. Indeed, as a multinational organization on par with the Church, their dissolution was inevitable. At this point, Templar gold and Templar ships disappeared. From then on only rumors remain, as Templar records were either destroyed or shipped out. But some Templars clearly visited the New World, since there are some archaeological artifacts and anomalies that indicate a knowledge of the New World such as those incorporated in Rosslyn Chapel's depiction of the corn plant (maize).

Enlightenment cities were designed using geometry and usually employed a grid broken up by angular boulevards. The idea was a break

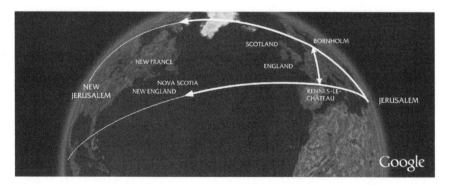

Figure 10.7. Extending the Bornholm and Rennes-le-Château 30° sector from Jerusalem into the New World. The United States is contained therein, a land built through Enlightenment thinking and founded on Scottish, French, and English Freemasonry.

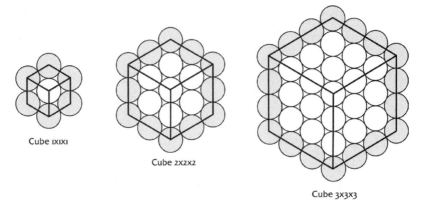

Cube ıxıxı

Cube 2x2x2

Cube 3x3x3

Figure 10.8. The development of the hexagonal numbers seven, nineteen, and thirty-seven. In the latter number, one can see the number of lunations in a three-year period, as well as the addition of eighteen and nineteen, which is the ratio between Saturn and Jupiter synods (see chapter 1).

with the incrementalism that so often plagued inner cities with narrow streets, higgledy piggledy styles from different ages—in a word, new thinking in layout but, alas, classicism writ large in the buildings themselves.

The New World offered great opportunities to build new cities from scratch and perhaps the greatest example is Washington, D.C., the capital of the fledgling United States that had just broken the yoke of Britain's colonial rule in 1776 and had a capital with a White House* by 1800. Rick Campbell and others provide the key to understanding the pattern found in Washington, D.C.[4] It requires a return to the traditions of Thoth and Michael, but in their Jewish form of Metatron's Cube.

The discipline of mathematics defines a style of number called a hexagonal number. The simplest of these is seven because six circles can be "packed" around a central circle to form six centers and a hexagon spreading out into space. To expand the pattern further requires twelve more circles around the outside to make a total of nineteen circles. Again, the pattern can be expanded to form thirty-seven by adding eighteen more circles (fig. 10.8). These are significant numbers.

Nineteen has been touted as the signature of the creator but the

---

*But not called that until the twentieth century.

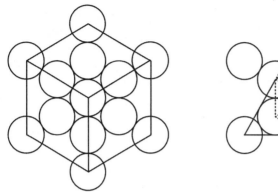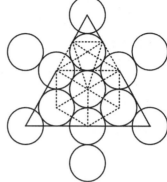

Figure 10.9. The creation of Metatron's Cube from the hexagonal number nineteen scales down into many self-similar patterns including, on the right, a smaller "cube" with a slightly distorted pentagram (five-sided star) above it.

middle figure can have six outer circles removed to form a very important figure in the development of the cubic altar tradition (alluded to in chapter 7): Metatron's Cube.

Equated with Michael, Grail lore, Melchizedek, and many other traditional archetypes, Metatron is again a facet of the Mercury (root three) function that transforms Earth especially through human agency. The name *Metatron* emerges largely by association with the biblical prophet Enoch, who was taken up to heaven and was clearly associated with the Sun. The Book of Enoch describes a temple made of "portals" that records the progress of the Sun's rising and setting positions for each month in the year, decoded by Robin Heath as located at the latitude of Stonehenge, *a portal temple.*

Thus, there is a connection between the Metatron of the Jewish prophets, prehistoric astronomy, and the northern latitudes, a fact that does not sit easily with conventional biblical history. This is similar, however, to the association of Apollo with Hyperborea and the "amber routes" from the Baltic. Just as medieval Christianity had its mystical secrets, the Jews must have had similar mysteries. It appears likely that, through the Templars, numerical secrets from prehistory survived and became operational again; geomantic landscape temples are indeed to be expected as the manifestation of this knowledge.

A NEW HOME IN THE NEW WORLD

Using this hypothesis, history can now be brought as near to the present as is probably comfortable, for Campbell identifies the street plan of Washington, D.C., as that of Metatron's cube, a pretty unlikely and inexplicable fact, given that no explanation of the design is available. Washington therefore represents a living manifestation of the ancient ideas forming a landscape temple in use down to the present day. The White House forms its center (fig. 10.10).

It is the metrology of the pattern that reveals something harking back to the past. The front of the cube appears as a major dimension and certainly cuts a long story short since its side length, the distance from the White House to the Jefferson Memorial, is one royal mile—exactly the distance of the Royal Mile in Edinburgh. The royal mile is a prehistoric measure of Earth, 8/7 English miles long. It perfectly divides, and therefore *represents,* the polar radius of Earth, which is 3,456 such miles long (fig. 10.11).

While the Jefferson Memorial to White House distance is one royal mile, the pyramid base, at right angles to it, is almost exactly pi royal miles. This is the circumference of a circle with a one royal mile diameter. Therefore, if pi equal to 22/7 were used, as it was in prehistory, then pi times one is 22/7 royal miles; since the true pyramid is eleven base to seven height, then 22/7 divided by eleven gives a unit length of 2/7 and multiplying by seven reveals that a Giza-like pyramid with this base would have a height of exactly two royal miles (fig. 10.12).

Figure 10.12 shows the true pyramid with its apex two royal miles above the common base. This apex is a hidden aspect of the design. At the top of this pyramid sits the Masonic temple of the 33° Supreme Council (Scottish Rite), east of 16th Street.

The profile of the Great Pyramid, available in John Greaves' sketch of 1646 or possibly from esoteric sources, appears to have been harmonized with the Metatronic pattern of the western part of the city. The Eye in the Pyramid is a major icon of the United States, shown on the reverse of its Great Seal and then on its currency, and it appears to be symbolic of the Supreme Council.

Figure 10.10. *The manifestation of Metatron in the layout of Washington, D.C., in which major and familiar monuments and boulevards follow the pattern, albeit adapted to the topography and incorporating the Renaissance technique of perspective.*

Figure 10.11. The key measure in the Washington pattern appears to be the royal mile between the White House and the Jefferson Memorial, shown here with a pair of Masonic dividers at their classic angle, the axle of which is the Capitol Building.

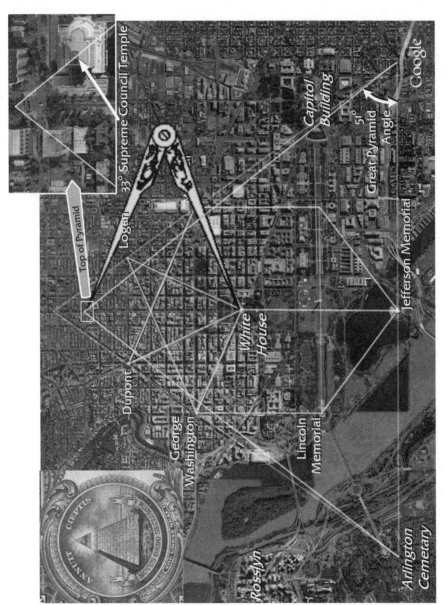

Figure 10.12. The Eye in the Pyramid symbol within the Great Seal and the Washington layout. The dividers shown in figure 10.11 can be seen as the boulevards that travel between the White House, Capitol Hill, and the Jefferson Memorial.

This pattern of Metatron's cube appears to have arisen out of nowhere as a new root three geometry used in the layout of Washington, D.C. However, John Michell[5] reveals the same pattern without identifying it in the most familiar of spiritual centers, the old town of Jerusalem, the very same place where the Knights Templar are suspected to have found the secrets of the Temple of Solomon. Michell provides us with a link between Jerusalem and Washington that, as we see later, could make Washington a candidate for the New Jerusalem, of which much has been said in the Bible and in the three main religions based upon the patriarchs of the Bible. "New Jerusalem is the concept of Jerusalem being renewed or rebuilt, either in the present day or in the future, either at the Temple Mount or in a different location."[6]

Given that the street plan of Jerusalem is said by Michell to be six times the likely plan of the Temple of Solomon, then the technique of using streets in cities to hold a geomantic pattern has its clear precedent in this case. We know that ancient cities were designed geomantically and relative to the sky and latitude, whereas we consider streets to be modern constructions and do not see them as carriers of sightlines and alignments in the prehistoric sense, within the modern built heritage. The interest of enlightenment thinkers in city plans should come as no shock but it has been hidden from view, like the wood hiding the trees.

Most of the streets of Jerusalem follow an approximate grid pattern, but in the north the Damascus Gate has a focus of roads that had led, just inside the gate, to Hadrian's column, erected by the Roman emperor of that name. These streets, like some boulevards of Washington, break the grid at multiples of 18 degrees, the angle of the pentagon star (fig. 10.13).

The New Jerusalem is described in the Book of Revelations in verses 3:12 and 21:2 and then in 21:16 as being a cube sized twelve units by twelve units by twelve units, in thousands of stadia where a stadium is 600 feet long. This cube would equal half the volume of the Moon; accordingly, for city plans, models of the New Jerusalem must suffice— or is this information *coded* in some way?

It is impossible to know whether Jerusalem had such city planning before the Crusades. However, since the street plan of Jerusalem has

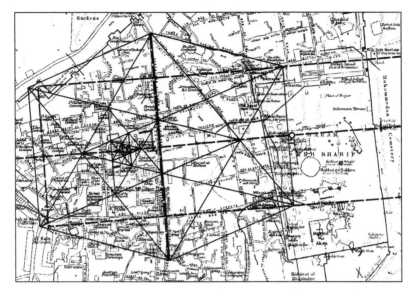

Figure 10.13. John Michell's discovery of Metatron's cube in Jerusalem, reconstructed by following the lead of thirty-six degree—that is, pentagonal—geometry in some of the roads radiating from the Damascus Gate. (From The Temple at Jerusalem: A Revelation *by John Michell, 2000.)*

remained hidden at least since then, the plan represents a marker for tracing its secret use in the layout of Washington. This is very important as it is the first actual, traceable information or artifact that can be said to originate in Jerusalem as a possible secret of the Knights Templar and their secret history in the West.

Returning to the D.C. pattern, the pentagons of Jerusalem shown in figure 10.13 can be drawn in and the Pentagon over the river shown in its alignment to the overall pattern (fig. 10.14).

These parts of the pattern were completed in the twentieth century, around the time of the Second World War, whereupon the United States took on the mantle of an economic and military superpower.

A NEW HEAVEN AND A NEW EARTH

The combination of Templar knowledge, their likely flight to the New World, their development of the first multinational bank, the history

Figure 10.14. The pentagons within the cube with a circle of one royal mile around the White House. The Jefferson Monument projects the base of the cube to locate the Pentagon while the alignment of the Pentagon is chosen with one point facing the White House at thirty degrees from north.

and flag of Switzerland,* known for its banking, their need for secrecy and belief in things not acceptable to orthodox Christianity and so on, has rightly lead to the simplifying assumption that the Knights Tem-

---

*Switzerland was made up of about one third of the older Burgundian kingdom and hence was a natural place for the Knights Templar to re-group when they went underground, while their ships became involved in exploration and piracy. The flag of Switzerland, inverse of the Templar smock, is the only square flag apart from that of the Vatican. The skull and crossbones on the pirate flag used a motif familiar to crusading knights who, if they died, would be rendered down so that just their bones could be returned home efficiently. Such symbols become all-important to secret societies who cannot declare themselves directly, the crossed bones are a common motif in Masonic graveyards, for example.

plar were transformed through the periods of the Reformation and the Enlightenment into new forms of secret society. The Freemasons, who established the United States, were one such group.

The design of Metatron's cube was fundamental to the esoteric core of the temple building found in the books of the prophets in the Bible and it is identified with Enoch in his ascended form. It is highly likely that the Knights Templar, if they discovered something of power or significance from Jewish sources, could have found this same pattern. Elements of it have been found in Jerusalem, utilizing the street plan, and this same New Jerusalem pattern became a template for city and state building in Washington, D.C.

There was evidently still a metrological basis to New World geomancy. The royal mile employed as a primary measure has a clear relation to the Pole. The pyramid of two such miles divides the Pole "perfectly" 1,728 times, that is as twelve times twelve times twelve or twelve cubed. Could this be the biblical New Jerusalem said, in Revelations 21:16, to be twelve cubed in size?

We note that for Washington 6,000 *root* English feet times 176/175 equals a royal mile. Thus the reciprocal is true that two royal miles are 12,000 *canonical* English feet (176/175 or 1.0057 times the standard English foot).* It appears then that "thousands of feet" equates to "thousands of stadia" in Revelations 21:16. This sort of distortion is often found in ancient documents where, for example, lunations or days were meant but years were stated.

In this case, as with the Great Pyramid, the two royal mile cube can be seen as being a unique geodetic structure. While its sides divide into Earth's pole 1,728 or 12^3 times, at the same time its dimensions are twelve kilofeet, of the canonical variety, so that its volume would then be 1,728 kilofeet cubed. This demonstrates again the unique position of the English foot in metrology in that it also divides up the equator (solar year times 360,000 feet) and the mean Earth radius ($12^6 \times 7$ feet) in meaningful ways.

---

*It is hard to understand these sorts of transformations. A royal mile is 8/7 of 5,280 root English feet. Thus, when measuring it with the slightly longer root canonical foot, it becomes exactly 6,000 feet long rather than 6,034.2857 root English feet.

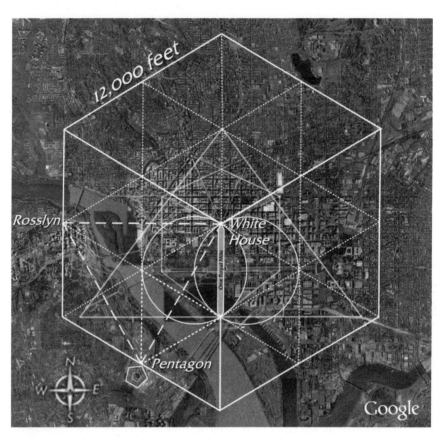

Figure 10.15. Constructing a two royal mile cube as the New Jerusalem. The high ground of Rosslyn was probably used as a primary surveying point but the isometric grid, as at Bornholm, is thirty degrees relative to the Rosslyn to White House, east–west line that is root three of a royal mile long within the cube. The Great Pyramid outline has its apex on the crossing within the cube's top face.

Finally, the number twelve has been noted as a marker for the Indo-European culture, and the Pentagon to White House bearing, at thirty degrees east of north, gives a sector of twelve-foldness that creates an isometric grid revealing the cube of New Jerusalem.

It is particularly relevant to trace the evolution of the landscape temple of Washington, D.C. This symbolism could have involved astrological sightlines as suggested by David Ovason in *The Secret Zodiacs of Washington D.C.*,[7] however, using sacred geometry instead Nicholas Mann reveals important tensions between the application of the Golden

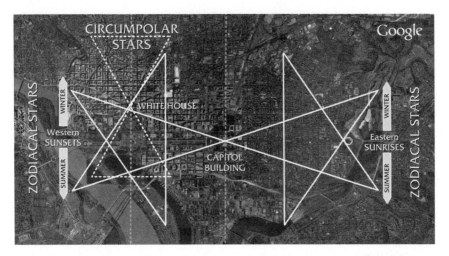

Figure 10.16. Washington, D.C., as an astronomical observatory in the megalithic style. L'Enfant's boulevards proposed a natural relationship to sky and Earth while integrating sacred number within the design. The Capitol is a symbol of solar rulership and the White House of polar rulership.

Mean in the original city design and the Metatronic pattern around the White House.[8]

From our reading of Nicholas Mann's account, three building styles emerge. The "ad rectangulum" of the Romanesque can be inferred in the grid iron pattern already employed in Philadelphia and apparently preferred by Thomas Jefferson. However, it was President Washington who appointed Major Pierre Charles L'Enfant (1754–1825) to design the city as a whole, and it was L'Enfant who superimposed, on the rectangular grid, angular boulevards secretly based upon a Golden Mean design, revealed clearly by Mann. This design could be called "ad pentangulum," something new—or perhaps very old?

The design was oriented to the eastern sunrise giving the boulevards the natural solar alignments to east and west remarked on by Ovason. However, L'Enfant also installed an equilateral triangle (i.e., the "ad triangulum" of the Medieval) north of the President's house (fig. 10.16). It was part of a one-royal-mile-high lattice that included the site of the Jefferson Memorial, which at that time lay beneath the Potomac River. Others precipitously took over control of L'Enfant's plan and the north–south meridional dimension was further evolved, as a *polar symbolism* focused on the White House. A new prime meridian was established by President Jefferson's "pier," replacing that established by L'Enfant through the Capitol building. The Metatronic pattern, visible from the air today, is therefore the result of these and other changes in emphasis. However, L'Enfant had already used the Royal mile, a polar measure, as the northern dimension in his design and much of his pentangular design for the boulevards also remains intact.[9]

This makes the Federal City the most ambitious expression of sacred city design undertaken, incorporating as it does so much of the sacred number and geomantic traditions that we have termed Atlantean. L'Enfant was a Frenchman from enlightenment Paris and was probably the most successful architect in post-revolutionary America. What School could have prepared this man, called "the child," to have delivered such a master class in harmonization of 2, 3, and 5, the first three prime numbers, at this great moment of opportunity? Could he be the link to the possible descendants of the Templars, the Society of

Figure 10.17. The Washington National Monument in the context of the White House, looking northwest. (Courtesy of Wikimedia Commons.)

St. Sulpice, the Compagnie du Saint-Sacrement that set up Monreal, the Jacobites in Paris, or even a real Prieure de Sion?

The original city design had a column one mile *east* of the Capitol. The later focus on the *western* city led eventually to some further metrology and polar symbolism, within the Washington National Monument beside a meridian that would come to define the centre of the City and of America.

THE WASHINGTON NATIONAL MONUMENT

As this monument evolved from foundation to final realization, its location was moved a small distance from the White House meridian. A pyramid rather than a five pointed star was placed upon its top and its shape became tapered to approach the form of an Egyptian obelisk. The height, to the base of the raised pyramid, was eventually set at 500 feet and its proportions then defined by the rules set for ancient obelisks. The small pyramid on top was given, like the pyramid on the reverse of the Great Seal design, thirteen courses of masonry, and the pyramidion capping was made of aluminum, then a rare and non-traditional metal.[10]

The base is square having a side length of fifty-five and one eighth feet (Parks Department figure). This is very interesting since the odd one eighth of a foot divided into the side length equals 441 units, the designed full height of the Great Pyramid in Sumerian feet. (In standard English feet the side length is of course 440 units.) Within the constraints of the monument's perimeter size, the extra eighth has allowed the Earth's Mean radius to Polar radius to be represented as 55.125 to 55 feet.[11]

> *We shall not cease from exploration*
> *And the end of all our exploring*
> *Will be to arrive where we started*
> *And know the place for the first time.*
>   T. S. ELIOT

POSTSCRIPT

The dichotomy raised in this book between ancient knowledge and its continuing but secret life within modern society has been shown to be more than of academic interest only. It is a primary unexplained aspect of the modern world that deserves far more study and far less sensationalism.

While the outer culture has developed an idea of personal freedom, increasing mechanisms of control are growing as the world state of nations is consolidating its growth. At the same time, the role of secret groups is becoming more clear. Their inherent threat to democracy has to be weighed against the fact that democracy was invented in Athens by "men from the north," and that secret groups through the Enlightenment tried to reduce the power of the Church and of kings, which both impeded democracy's growth.

This raises a question about the evolution of humanity and whether— if Earth is actually being evolved by spiritual forces—knowledge of these forces and the sacred geometry associated with them should again become known, so that the general population might again interact with the planet as spiritual, rather than "having a religion," "making money," or "believing in technology." This might be possible again if the planet is emerging from a human dark age.

APPENDIX ONE

ASTROPHYSICAL CONSTANTS

ASTROPHYSICAL CONSTANTS

Lunar Year	354.367 days (12 lunations)
Eclipse Year	346.62 days
Lunar Node Period	18.618 years or 6800 days
Moon's Radius	1083 miles (ancient value = 1080 miles)

	SYNODIC	SIDEREAL	
	(DAYS)	(DAYS)	(YEARS)
Mercury	115.88	87.969	0.24085
Venus	583.92	224.701	0.61521
Earth	365.242199	365.256	1.00004
Moon	29.53059	27.32166	
Mars	779.94	686.980	1.88089
Jupiter	398.88	4332.589	11.86223
Saturn	378.09	10759.22	29.4577

A BRIEF INTRODUCTION TO THE METROLOGY OF NEAL AND MICHELL

There used to be an interest in metrology, especially in the study of ancient monuments. However the information revealed from sites often became mixed with the religious ideas of the researcher, leading to coding systems such as those of pyramidology and gematria. The general effect has been that metrology, outside of modern engineering uses, has been left unconsidered by modern scientific archaeology.

Metrology seemed a very complex subject before John Neal and John Michell redefined it in a very compelling and much simpler fashion. The ancient measures were first found in different regions of the world and so became known by the name of a civilization or country. This implied and later led to the assumption that these measures had been uniquely developed in those regions in an arbitrary fashion.

But ancient measures are not arbitrary and indeed are all related to a single and unified system. This simplicity would have been obvious had measures not been slightly "varied," for precise reasons. Aside from these variations, John Neal has identified that the English foot is the basis of the whole system—used as the number one within it—and all the other types of foot are, at root, rationally related using integer fractions of an English foot. What might appear to be a rather partisan approach should be understood in the knowledge that the English foot did not come from England.

It is also important to base such a discussion on the length naturally called "foot" since, while it is only one of many longer and shorter units of length, each such greater length is simply made up of feet according to a formula. Subdividing a foot can yield ten, twelve, sixteen, or other divisions, such as inches or digits, in different measures. A yard is generally three feet and a pace two and a half. All of the different feet appear to lie within a given range, plus or minus, of the English foot.

Because the ancient feet largely use low numbers in their fractions of the English and most often are superparticular (where the denominator and numerator vary by one as in 8/7, the royal foot), many of them represent musical tones; the measures are interrelated in the same ratios found in musical harmony (chapter 2). This is shown in figure A.1 but has not been an important consideration so far in applying this metrological system.

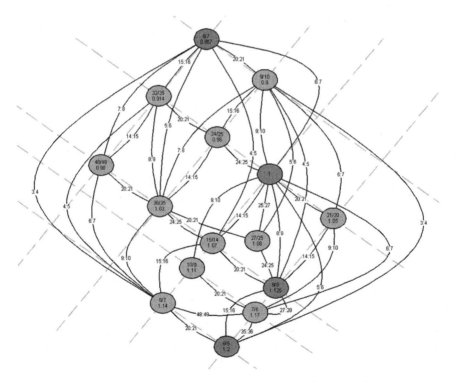

Figure A.1. The net of harmonious measure: harmonic relations within measures.

THE TWELVE MAIN MEASURES

There are twelve main measures and usually any measure found is a variation (see later) of one of these rather than the root value. Each root value forms what is called a *module*. Neal and Michell have identified twelve modules:[1]

MODULE	RELATION TO ENGLISH FOOT	NOTES
Assyrian Foot	9/10 = 0.9 ft	When cubits achieve a length of 1.8 ft such as the Assyrian cubit they are divisible by two, instead of the 1 ½ ft division normally associated with the cubit length. Variations of this measure are distinctively known as *Oscan, Italic,* and *Mycenaean* measure.
Iberian Foot	32/35 = 0.9142857 ft	This is the foot of 1/3 of the Spanish *vara*, which survived as the standard of Spain from prehistory to the present.
Roman Foot	24/25 = 0.96 ft	Most who are interested in metrology would consider this value to be too short as a definition of the Roman foot, but examples survive as rulers very accurately at this length.
Common Egyptian Foot	48/49 = 0.979592 ft	One of the better-known measures, being six sevenths of the royal Egyptian foot.
English/Greek Foot	1 ft	The English foot is one of the variations of what are accepted as Greek measure, variously called Olympian or Geographic.
Common Greek Foot	36/35 = 1.028571 ft	This was a very widely used module recorded throughout Europe; it survived in England at least until the reforms of Edward I in 1305. It is also the *half sacred Jewish cubit* upon which Newton pondered and Berriman referred to it as *cubit A*.

MODULE (CONT.)	RELATION TO ENGLISH FOOT (CONT.)	NOTES (CONT.)
Persian Foot	21/20 = 1.05 ft	Half the Persian cubit of Darius the Great. Reported in its variations throughout the Middle East, North Africa and Europe, survived as the *Hashimi* foot of the Arabian league and the *pied de roi* of the Franks.
Belgic Foot	15/14 = 1.071428 ft	Develops into the *Drusian foot* or foot of the *Tungri*. Detectable in many megalithic monuments.
Sumerian Foot	12/11 = 1.097142 ft	Perhaps the most widely dispersed module of all, recorded throughout Europe, Asia, and North Africa, commonly known as the *Saxon* or *Northern* foot.
Yard and Full Hand Foot	11/10 = 1.111111 ft	This is the foot of the 40 inch yard widely used in medieval England until suppressed by statute in 1439. It is the basis of *Punic* measure and variants are recorded in Greek statuary from Asia Minor.
Royal Egyptian Foot	8/7 = 1.142857 ft	The most discussed and scrutinized historical measurement. Examples of this length are plentiful.
Russian Foot	7/6 = 1.166666 ft	One half of the Russian *arshin*, one sixth of the *sadzhen*. One and one half of these feet as a cubit would be the *Arabic black cubit*, also the *Egyptian cubit of the Nilometer*.

To this list others can be added such as the Inverse Iberian Foot (35/32 = 1.09375 ft). This module, which is one part in 8000 different from the present meter, is found at Carnac. Another important measure is the Drusian Foot (27/25 = 1.08 ft).

THE ROLE OF ACCURACY AND VARIATIONS

One immediate problem with these measures appears to be their accuracy, as in the number of decimal places shown in the modules above. However, this is an artifact of the decimal system that only employs the two primes two and five, which constitute ten. The above modules are often rational fractions of an English foot involving other primes, notably three leading to 0.333333 . . . written as $0.\overline{3}$, using the overline to represent a repeating fraction. Seven in the denominator, as in 8/7, leads to the repeating fraction $1.\overline{142857}$ for the royal foot. The problem lies not in the number base used but rather in the accuracy of, say, the Roman foot at 0.96; it should be written 0.960000 or similarly to show that in practice the full fraction is shown, but the practice of metrology will always be measurable according to our instruments. Correcting a measurement to show the intent within the system is a movement toward the meaning of a monument such as, for example, that it represents the polar radius of Earth by employing a module with 11/7 in its mix of primes, in feet.

Each of the above types of foot measurement can be and are usually found *systematically* varied from the root values of the given module.

The first variation is by one or more applications of the ratio A = 176/175, which contains eleven above and seven below (also sixteen above and twenty-five below). The 11/7 allows the ratio to function in various ways:

1. It can resolve the difference between the diameter and circumference of a circle so that whole numbers of two different variations of the same module are present despite the fact that pi is irrational —because the accurate 22/7 approximation has 11/7 within it.
2. It can convert a module with no prime numbers apart from two, three, and five in it into a polar measure—a measure that divides into the polar radius of Earth.
3. Since the meridian of Earth between 10° and 51° generates a degree of latitude length that varies by this amount, then two measures differing by this ratio will divide the two latitudes to give the same count in feet.

This latter use was deduced by Michell, which led to his early categorization of measures as *Tropical* and *Northern,* the latter longer by a factor of 176/175. Analysis of the different historical measures led Neal to the simpler idea that a table of variations was involved, and that each module was based upon a simple fraction of the English foot.

The second ratio used for variation is B = 441/440, which is the ratio of Earth's mean radius to its polar radius, again discovered by Michell. It has seventy-two above and eleven below and can be used in similar ways to the first:

1. When suitably employed this ratio can resolve the difference between the diameter and circumference of a circle.
2. It can convert a module with seven in its denominator into a polar measure.
3. The meridian of Earth again generates degrees of latitude length that vary by this amount, so that two measures differing by this ratio will divide the two latitudes to give the same count in feet.

Thus, the two ratios used to vary measures were those that already related to the ellipse of the meridian, the size of Earth, and its deformation due to daily rotation.

Since the English foot is "one" for the system, then its own variations also demonstrate the grid ratios. Neal generates such a grid using 176/175 for horizontal differences and 441/440 for vertical ones, as in this table:

	LEAST	RECIPROCAL	ROOT	CANONICAL	GEOGRAPHIC
ROOT	0.98867	0.994318	1.0	1.0057143	1.0114612
STANDARD	0.990916	0.996578	1.002272	1.008	1.01376

- A = 176/175 = 1.0057143 and B = 441/440 = 1.002272
- 1.01376 is therefore one times A times A times B since two columns and one row are involved
- 0.98867 is 1/A^2

Other modules are then varied similarly, as in the case of the Persian Foot that is 21/20 feet long in its Root value.

	LEAST	RECIPROCAL	ROOT	CANONICAL	GEOGRAPHIC
ROOT	1.038102	1.044034	1.05	1.056	1.062034
STANDARD	1.040461	1.046406	1.052386	1.0584	1.064448

- 1.0644486 is therefore 1.05 times A times A times B since two columns and one row are involved.
- 1.038102 is $1.05/A^2$.

The names have come to be adopted out of experience but, having become part of a coherent system, they are then employed to communicate the variety of a given module. Thus, the foot behind the astronomical megalithic yard (AMY) of 19.008/7 feet is one third of this yard, which rationally is 792/875 feet. However, this foot is 176/175 times the Assyrian Foot of 9/10 or 0.9 feet. Thus it should be referred to as being a "root canonical Assyrian foot." The AMY is also a pace of two and a half feet if the Drusian foot of 27/25 is similarly varied, that is, a "pace of root canonical Drusian feet" could also describe it.

In practice tables can be prepared for reference or, as is more common, ad hoc calculations are done on a calculator to measure the variation of a *measurement* within a possible module. For instance: John James associated the Roman foot with Chartres in *The Master Masons of Chartres* (see chapter 8). He used a figure that was 6.8 feet to seven Roman feet, but this would not belong to ancient metrology for its formula would then contain the prime number 17. The nearest of Neal's values would be the *root geographical Roman foot* where the root value of 24/25 feet is increased twice by 176/175 to give 0.971003 feet, a difference of less than 0.04%.

OTHER METROLOGICAL SYSTEMS

A number of non-academic books incorporate some metrology while academic books are largely catalogues of historic values and approximate relationships between the above modules. Virtually nobody has adopted the system of Neal and Michell. What is generally found is at best sufficient for the work being done but more often is not ancient and interprets monuments in an eccentric fashion.

The Bronze Age Computer Disk by Alan Butler provides a typical example of how the coincidences within the numerical environment start to reveal facets of the ancient system. While it is possible that there were other, different metrological systems, the evidence points to a single system of measure wherever metrology has been employed. This is crucial: What must have been a thousand years in the making was the greatest cultural artifact ever created and was part of a worldview that was transmitted between antediluvian civilizations down to historical times. Most of the results developed in this book can only step beyond surmise because of this metrological system. Just as a new telescope can lead automatically to new knowledge of celestial objects and phenomena, the application of metrology to ancient sites appears to reveal interesting facts that cannot be seen otherwise. Almost all other lines of approach are hampered by the ravages of both time and later civilizations. When a metrological monument survives at all, its metrology usually survives intact and can be deduced from a knowledge of the measures used in the ancient world.

REFERENCE TABLE OF VARIED
ANCIENT MEASURES

Each type of foot generates modules of varied feet according to just two ratios, as explained above:

ASSYRIAN FOOT 9/10 = 0.9 FT

	LEAST	RECIPROCAL	ASSYRIAN	CANONICAL	GEOGRAPHIC
ROOT	0.889802	0.894886	0.900000	0.905143	0.910315
STANDARD	0.891824	0.896920	0.902045	0.907200	0.912384

IBERIAN FOOT 32/35 = .9142857 FT

	LEAST	RECIPROCAL	IBERIAN	CANONICAL	GEOGRAPHIC
ROOT	0.903926	0.909091	0.914286	0.919510	0.924765
STANDARD	0.905980	0.911157	0.916364	0.921600	0.926866

ROMAN FOOT 24/25 = .96 FT

	LEAST	RECIPROCAL	ROMAN	CANONICAL	GEOGRAPHIC
ROOT	0.949122	0.954545	0.960000	0.965486	0.971003
STANDARD	0.951279	0.956715	0.962182	0.967680	0.973210

COMMON EGYPTIAN FOOT 48/49 = 0.979592 FT

	LEAST	RECIPROCAL	COMMON EGYPTIAN	CANONICAL	GEOGRAPHIC
ROOT	0.968492	0.974026	0.979592	0.985190	0.990819
STANDARD	0.970693	0.976240	0.981818	0.987429	0.993071

THE ENGLISH AND GREEK FOOT 1 = 1.000000 FT

	LEAST	RECIPROCAL	ENGLISH	CANONICAL	GEOGRAPHIC
ROOT	0.988669	0.994318	1.000000	1.005714	1.011461
STANDARD	0.990916	0.996578	1.002273	1.008000	1.013760

COMMON GREEK FOOT 36/35 = 1.028571 FT

	LEAST	RECIPROCAL	COMMON GREEK	CANONICAL	GEOGRAPHIC
ROOT	1.016916	1.022727	1.028571	1.034449	1.040360
STANDARD	1.019227	1.025052	1.030909	1.036800	1.042725

PERSIAN FOOT 21/20 = 1.05 FT

	LEAST	RECIPROCAL	PERSIAN	CANONICAL	GEOGRAPHIC
ROOT	1.038102	1.044034	1.050000	1.056000	1.062034
STANDARD	1.040461	1.046407	1.052386	1.058400	1.064448

BELGIC FOOT 15/14 = 1.071428 FT

	LEAST	RECIPROCAL	BELGIC	CANONICAL	GEOGRAPHIC
ROOT	1.059288	1.065341	1.071429	1.077551	1.083708
STANDARD	1.061695	1.067762	1.073864	1.080000	1.086171

INVERSE IBERIAN FOOT 35/32 = 1.09375 FT

	LEAST	RECIPROCAL	CARNAC	CANONICAL	GEOGRAPHIC
ROOT	1.081356	1.087536	1.093750	1.100000	1.106286
STANDARD	1.083814	1.090007	1.096236	1.102500	1.108800

SUMERIAN FOOT 12/11 = 1.097142 FT

	LEAST	RECIPROCAL	SUMERIAN	CANONICAL	GEOGRAPHIC
ROOT	1.078548	1.084711	1.090909	1.097143	1.103412
STANDARD	1.080999	1.087176	1.093388	1.099636	1.105920

YARD AND FULL HAND FOOT 11/10 = 1.111111 FT

	LEAST	RECIPROCAL	YARD & HAND	CANONICAL	GEOGRAPHIC
ROOT	1.087536	1.093750	1.100000	1.106286	1.112607
STANDARD	1.090007	1.096236	1.102500	1.108800	1.115136

ROYAL EGYPTIAN FOOT 8/7 = 1.142857 FT

	LEAST	RECIPROCAL	ROYAL	CANONICAL	GEOGRAPHIC
ROOT	1.129907	1.136364	1.142857	1.149388	1.155956
STANDARD	1.132475	1.138946	1.145455	1.152000	1.158583

RUSSIAN FOOT 7/6 = 1.166666 FT

	LEAST	RECIPROCAL	RUSSIAN	CANONICAL	GEOGRAPHIC
ROOT	1.153447	1.160038	1.166667	1.173333	1.180038
STANDARD	1.156068	1.162674	1.169318	1.176000	1.182720

NOTES

INTRODUCTION: NUMBER AND CREATION

1. *Stonehenge, A Journey Back in Time* (Video; England: Cromwell/English Heritage, 1998).
2. See Giorgio De Santillana and Hertha Von Dechend, *Hamlet's Mill* (Jaffrey, N.H.: David R. Godine, 1977).

CHAPTER ONE: NUMBERS FROM THE SKY

1. Alexander Marshack, *The Roots of Civilization: The Cognitive Beginnings of Man's First Art, Symbol and Notation* (London: Weidenfeld and Nicolson, 1972).
2. See Robert Graves, *The Greek Myths* (London: Penguin Books, 1960), particularly "The Dethronement of Cronus," 7.1.

CHAPTER TWO: THE ROOT OF ALL MEASURES

1. ". . . the intervals which are most pleasing to the ear are those given by the simplest rational numbers . . . . Thus consonance is associated with the ratio of *small* integers. More precisely, natural ratios are of the form $2^p \times 3^q \times 5^r$ . . . the 7th and 11th harmonics always being excluded from consideration." From F. J. Budden, "Modern Mathematics and Music," *The Mathematical Gazette,* 19 Feb 1969.

CHAPTER THREE: THE MODEL OF EARTH

1. Discovered initially by John Michell in *Ancient Metrology* in 1982 (Bristol, England: Pentacle Books) and extended by John Neal in *All Done With Mirrors* by 2002 (London: Secret Academy).
2. Further elaboration can be found in appendix 2, as well as *Ancient Metrology* by John Michell (Bristol, England: Pentacle Books, 1982) and *All Done With Mirrors* by John Neal (London: Secret Academy, 2002).
3. John Michell, *Ancient Metrology* (Bristol, England: Pentacle, 1982).
4. From *Certaine Errors in Navigation Detected and Corrected* (London, 1610).
5. From C. W. Allen, *Astrophysical Quantities* (London: Athlone Press, 1976).

CHAPTER FOUR: ANCIENT THEME PARKS

1. John Michell, *City of Revelation* (London: Garnstone Press, 1972).
2. Our account draws upon *The Temple at Jerusalem: A Revelation* by John Michell (Glastonbury, England: Gothic Image Publications, 2000).
3. Robin Heath, *Sun, Moon and Stonehenge* (Cardigan: Bluestone Press, 1998) and *The Measure of Albion* (Cardigan: Bluestone Press, 2004).
4. Jurgen Spanuth, *Atlantis of the North* (London: Sidgwick and Jackson, 1979).
5. John Michell, *Ancient Metrology* (Bristol, England: Pentacle, 1982) and John Neal, *All Done With Mirrors* (London: Secret Academy, 2002).
6. Robin Heath, *Sun, Moon and Stonehenge* (Cardigan: Bluestone Press, 1998).
7. Robin Heath and John Michell, *The Measure of Albion* (Cardigan: Bluestone, 2004).
8. This section is based on John Michell's presentation of the matter in *The Measure of Albion*.
9. Alexander Thom, *Megalithic Remains in Britain and Brittany* (Oxford: Oxford University Press, 1978).
10. Alexander Thom, *Megalithic Sites in Britain* (Oxford: Oxford University Press, 1967).
11. Adapted from Alexander Thom, *Megalithic Remains in Britain and Brittany* (Oxford: Oxford University Press, 1978).
12. Association Archeologique Kergal Booklet 20: *An Approach to Megalithic Geography.*
13. Robin Heath, *Sun, Moon and Stonehenge* (Cardigan: Bluestone Press, 1998).

CHAPTER FIVE: MYTHIC HEROES AND GEOMANTIC TECHNOLOGIES

1. The primary reference for this remains *Hamlet's Mill* by Santillana and Dechend.
2. From Peter Stewart, *The Architecture of the Spirit* (Rochester, Vt.: Inner Traditions, forthcoming 2007). See www.mythofcreation.co.uk.
3. John Michell, *At the Center of the World* (London: Thames & Hudson, 1994).
4. Earnest McClain, *The Pythagorean Plato* (New York: Nicolas-Hays, 1984).
5. Earnest McClain, *The Myth of Invariance* (New York: Nicolas-Hays, 1985).
6. Jean Richer, *Sacred Geography of the Ancient Greeks* (New York: SUNY, 1994).
7. By Lucien Richer in a development of his brother's work, originally in the French magazine *Atlantis* but translated in the pamphlet, *The St. Michael-Apollo 'Axis'—A Study in Sacred Geography* (Gatekeeper Trust, 1998).
8. Paul Broadhurst et al., *The Dance of the Dragon* (Cornwall: Mythos Books, 2000).
9. David Ulansey, *The Origins of the Mithraic Mysteries* (Oxford University Press, 1991).

CHAPTER SIX: SECRET MEN FROM THE NORTH

1. As described in Jean Richer, *Sacred Geography of the Ancient Greeks* (New York: SUNY, 1994).
2. "Geo-Physics and Human History: New Light on Plato's Atlantis and the Exodus," *Systematics* 1:2 (September 1963).
3. "The Hyperborean Origin of the Indo-European Culture," *Systematics* 1:3 (December 1963).

CHAPTER SEVEN: ANGELS OF THE TRANSFINITE

1. Discussed in J. G. Bennett, *The Dramatic Universe,* vol. 2 (London: Hodder & Stoughton, 1961), 244. He went on to use an even higher transfinite number, *Aleph Two,* as a means to think of the divine world as an unfathomable source of relatedness. See his later talks: *Creation* by J. G. Bennett (Santa Fe: Bennett Books, 1998).
2. Richard Heath, *Matrix of Creation* (Rochester, Vt.: Inner Traditions, 2004), 38–40.
3. Robert K. G. Temple, *Oracles of the Dead* (Rochester, Vt.: Destiny Books, 2005).
4. Stuart McHardy, *The Quest for the Nine Maidens* (Edinburgh, Scotland: Luath Press, 2002).
5. This is brought out in Gordon Strachan's *Chartres: Sacred Geometry, Sacred Space* (Edinburgh, Scotland: Floris Books, 2003).

CHAPTER EIGHT: THE TEMPLE'S LAST STAND

1. Jeanine Miller, *The Vision of Cosmic Order in the Vedas* (London: Routledge, Kegan & Paul, 1985), 93.

CHAPTER NINE: LIFE, THE UNIVERSE, AND EVERYTHING

1. Collins Pocket Dictionary, 1989.
2. J. G. Bennett, *The Dramatic Universe,* vol. 2: Foundations of Moral Philosophy (Charlestown, W.Va.: Claymont Communcations, 1961), 46.
3. J. G. Bennett, *The Dramatic Universe,* vol. 3: Man and His Nature (Charlestown, W.Va.: Claymont Communications, 1966).

CHAPTER TEN: BUILDING THE NEW JERUSALEM

1. Erling Haagensen and Henry Lincoln, *The Templars' Secret Island* (Gloucestershire, UK: Windrush Press, 2000), chapter 3.
2. As described in John Michell, *At the Center of the World* (London: Thames & Hudson, 1994).
3. Erling Haagensen and Henry Lincoln, *The Templars' Secret Island,* 50.
4. See Rick Campbell's website: www.geocities.com/jussaymoe/dc_symbolism/index.htm.
5. John Michell, *The Temple at Jerusalem: A Revelation* (York Beach, Me.: Weiser, 2000).
6. Wikipedia entry for New Jerusalem.
7. David Ovason, *The Secret Zodiacs of Washington D.C.* (London: Arrow Books, 2000).
8. Nicholas R. Mann, *The Sacred Geometry of Washington, D.C.* (Somerset, England: Green Magic, 2006).
9. Ibid.
10. For the full story of obelisks from ancient times, their connections with enlightenment groups, and the wonderful story of the building of the Washington Monument read *The Magic of Obelisks* by Peter Thomkins (New York: Harper & Row, 1981).
11. Thanks to John Neal for alerting me to this way into the coding of the base of the monument.

APPENDIX TWO: A BRIEF INTRODUCTION TO THE METROLOGY OF NEAL AND MICHELL

1. Table taken from John Neal, "Ancient Measurement Systems, Their fractional integration" (unpublished essay, 2004).

INDEX